CONSPIRACY OF ONE

The Definitive Book On The
Kennedy Assassination
JIM MOORE

CONSPIRACY OF ONE

The Definitive Book On The
Kennedy Assassination

JIM MOORE

THE SUMMIT GROUP
FORT WORTH, TEXAS

Published, 1990, in the United States of America by
The Summit Group
1227 West Magnolia, Fort Worth, Texas.
Published in 1990, this edition is unabridged and unaltered.

International Standard Book Number: 0-9626219-2-7

Manufactured in the United States of America
© 1990 by The Summit Group
1227 West Magnolia
Fort Worth, Texas 76104

Conspiracy Of One

For My Grandmother:
In her heart he still lived;
the Watchman of Honor
who did not sleep.

And for my wife, Kathy
who alone knows the cost.

In another recent book on the Kennedy assassination, Texas journalist Jim Marrs asks his readers not to trust what he has written. *Crossfire* further adds the admonition not to trust any book written on the killing of the President.

I can understand the injunction when it is applied to critics'* books which, in my opinion, are filled with supposition and woefully light on cold, hard facts. But I can say with great candor that *Conspiracy Of One* is one book you can and should believe.

There are five reasons why. First, I have spent the last 23 years researching my subject. I am not a Johnny-come-lately to the assassination investigation. Additionally, my training as a historian allows me to view objectively the evidence and contradictions in this case and render a sound judgment on their relative value.

Second, I have no axe to grind. I began as a critic, and I have progressed through their ranks. The fact that I now believe the so-called "official version" of the assassination should indicate to even the casual reader that I have come full circle. I am, therefore, intimately familiar with the arguments the critics use and the methods they employ in their quest for public attention and personal gain.

Third, my book deals with nothing but evidence, while most others on the

---

*Throughout Conspiracy Of One *I refer to the detractors of the official assassination story as "critics."*

subject deal with nothing but innuendo. This is a universal truth; the evidence in this case does nothing but strengthen the lone-assassin theory. Critics are hard-pressed to ignore it, but ignore it they do; the aforementioned *Crossfire* contains less than half-a-dozen pages detailing the medical evidence in this case. The other 575 pages are filled with a sort of literary grasping at straws.

Fourth, I do not accept the government-sponsored version of the assassination in its entirety. I believe the assassination of President Kennedy was no more than we were told it was, but I maintain that the details differ greatly from the official version. Thus, this book is not a rubber stamp for the Warren Commission. It merely picks up where the Commission and the House Select Committee on Assassinations left off years ago.

Fifth, and most importantly, this book names names and produces evidence—something no Warren Commission critic has ever done. Since my final solution does not correspond to the Warren Commission version of what happened that day in Dallas, it is as novel as one that propounds a gunman atop the grassy knoll in Dealey Plaza. The difference you must consider is that I have taken pains to prove each point I've made herein, while most critics substantiate their questions with more questions.

Considering Marrs' injunction, that you not believe this book, I think it only proper to add a few injunctions of my own. First, that you readers approach *Conspiracy Of One* with an open mind. This is a critical initial step.

I cannot count the individuals who have talked with me as I worked on the "Sixth Floor" exhibit in downtown Dallas and suggested that, since I did not believe in a conspiracy, I was not in full possession of the facts. Equally numberless are the times I was moved to reply that, having spent some 23 years researching the subject, I felt in full command of the evidence and testimony. I daresay the individuals to whom this remark was addressed had spent significantly less time drawing their pro-conspiracy conclusions.

An open mind, then, should be my readers' stock in trade. Quite plainly, there are very few individuals on the face of the earth who have more knowledge of the Kennedy assassination than I do. Unless you are one of those three or four, you owe it to yourself to keep an open mind as you begin this book.

If you find yourself unable to begin this book without a preconceived conclusion in mind, you have done two things. First, you have wasted your money, because nothing I say in *Conspiracy Of One* will make a difference to you. Second, you have cheated yourself, because the truth about the assassination is easily understood and accepted—if you are open-minded to absorbing it.

The second injunction I'd make is to ask you readers to read the book in sequence, as it was written. Reading *The Final Solution* first, for example, will only frustrate you because it relies on the previous medical evidence chapters as its base in fact. Take your time and be patient. You and I have waited 27 years for the answer to the crime of the century, and another few hours won't matter greatly.

Third, realize that the critics of the Warren Commission Report have not done us any favors. Indeed, they have managed to convince the majority of the American public that their institutions of government are not to be trusted. Had Oswald escaped the Dallas police on November 22, 1963, and lived to shoot Presidents Johnson, Nixon, Ford, Carter and Reagan, the damage would not have equalled what the critics have done to us during the past three decades.

Fourth, when in doubt, investigate. If you don't believe me when I tell you that a Carcano cartridge case can be dented by inserting it empty into the rifle chamber, go out and find a Carcano and an empty cartridge and see for yourself. If you don't believe that the so-called "pristine bullet," Commission Exhibit 399, is not pristine but quite flattened at the base, go to the National Archives and look for yourself. In a word, do the work. Do not decry the truth just because you are unwilling to go and look for yourself.

And fifth, hold other writers similarly accountable. Reading *Crossfire*, for example, you'll find this sentence: "Or do you believe witnesses who saw a rifle fired at Kennedy's right front and films that show the rearward fall of the wounded president indicating just such a shot?"

Marrs should know that there are no witnesses who saw a rifle being fired at Kennedy from any place other than the Texas School Book Depository building. He also should know that there are logical, scientific explanations for the rearward movement of the President's head after the fatal impact. If he claims otherwise, you should ask him to provide the proof. Perhaps the fact that he left the proof out of his book was just an oversight on his part.

You readers face a formidable task. I've given you five sound reasons why you should believe *Conspiracy Of One*, and asked you to pause to consider five injunctions before you begin to read the book. In a word, this book will make you work for the truth. However, it's my belief that the truth is a valuable-enough commodity to deserve a bit of your effort on its behalf.

I wrote this book for a single reason—to rid myself of the obsession that has dogged me through every phase of my life since I was a child. With the manuscript finished, and most of the details done, I still cannot abandon the path I have followed for so long.

Unfortunately, there can be no sequel to the unvarnished truth, and hence, none to this book. I'll keep digging, looking for additional proof that my final solution is really the most valid hypothesis that can be created. If I find something contrary to what I now believe, I hope that I have the fortitude to let you know that I was wrong. But that's something I don't anticipate having to deal with.

Much to the critics' dismay, I intend to be a thorn in their side for a long time to come. Bringing the truth about President Kennedy's assassination to light is a responsibility someone had to shoulder and that someone is me.

As Jack himself noted, "I do not shrink from this responsibility, I welcome it."

– *Jim Moore, Waco, Texas, Summer 1990*

A C K N O W L E D G E M E N T S

FOR ANY PROJECT OF THIS SCOPE AND MAGNITUDE, *there are dozens of individuals to thank. Without their help, I can truthfully say that this book would never have been written.*

Conover Hunt, the embattled Project Director for the Sixth Floor exhibit, has always been helpful and direct in guiding my research efforts. The time I spent working with her was well-spent indeed. Although she may not agree with my final solution to the assassination, I know that I will always have her as a friend at the bar of history.

Carl Henry is perhaps as patient and non-judgmental a researcher as any I've met. Always kind to me, Carl gave me much food for thought while I wrote this book. I appreciate his willingness to listen, and I admire his ability to withhold judgment.

Rick Lane, the Dallas box manufacturer who helped me begin the reconstruction of the corner window and the corner stairway areas in the Sixth Floor exhibit, has become a good friend and a great client. Rick fabricated the hundreds of boxes we used in the re-creation, and I admire his skill.

Lindalyn Adams and the staff at the Dallas County Historical Foundation have been most kind, even when the hour was late and the days hot and long. I appreciate their trust and belief in my potential, for without access to the creative sessions that actually formed the Sixth Floor exhibit, this book would not have become a reality. I especially want to thank Dave, Sheryl, and V'Ann for all they've done on my behalf.

For a decade and a half I've talked on a continuing basis with assassination witnesses and those closest to the event. Most have been unfailingly kind. I especially want to thank Phil and Marilyn Willis for inviting me into their home and for sharing their memories with me. Also, thanks to Marina Oswald Porter for our brief conversations. Many of the witnesses I talked to years ago have left an impact on me. I hope that, through this book, I have left their legacy to the world.

David Belin and John Lattimer were always willing to spend time with me on the telephone, answering questions about the assassination, the investigations, and the evidence. I deeply and sincerely appreciate their desire to help set the record straight.

The staff (my friends and co-workers) at Success Motivation Institute helped me past some of the hurdles I had to overcome in order to produce this manuscript. I especially want to thank Jim and Judy Sirbasku for their friendship, John Mills and Bud Haney for their guidance, and John Robison for his poor attempts at humor.

A special thanks to my secretary, Kelly Hlavenka, for placing and answering the dozens of calls during the preparation of this book. Her attention to detail was truly above and beyond the call of duty.

My parents, Bill and JoAnn Moore, have always been wise enough to encourage my rather unusual interests, even though it meant interrupting their personal lives. Though I haven't always shown it, I deeply appreciate their support and effort.

If I could touch the Elysian Fields with the written word, I would give special thanks to my great-grandfather, N.O. Kenner. Not only was he the wisest man I have ever met, but he awakened in me the desire to always want to know more. Without the opportunity to know and learn from him, this book would never have been written. He was the first person to believe in me and my potential, and I miss him deeply.

This is not an easy book to publish in 1990. I am especially grateful to Mark Hulme and the Summit Group—my deepest thanks to Kirby Faulk, Starlette Pickett, Cheryl Corbitt, and the Creative Team.

These pages comprise the beginning and the end of my sentimentality. As my college writing instructor once told me, writing is serious business.

JIM MOORE

IT ALWAYS HAPPENED. On the sixth floor of the old Texas School Book Depository, as we worked on the Sixth Floor Exhibit, or over lunch at one of the area restaurants, Jim Moore and I were once again locked in thoughtful debate over topics pertaining to the assassination of President John F. Kennedy.

You could not find two more disparate points of view on some topics of conversation, or two that were more in line on other interest areas. Jim and I have had an ongoing discussion concerning the assassination of President Kennedy since the day we met in 1988 on the fifth floor of the Depository in the office of Conover Hunt, Project Director of the Sixth Floor Exhibit. Back and forth, round and round, over the last two years, Jim and I have examined every blade of grass and the twig of every tree in Dealey Plaza. From plotting out the location and angles of shots fired from the sixth floor window to standing (hopefully) in the exact spot where witnesses stood and trying to understand what they could (and could not) have seen, I have had the time and opportunity to come to know and appreciate Jim Moore.

When Jim asked that I write this introduction, I jumped at the chance because I believe that he and I share the same heartfelt concern.

Over the past few years, objective rational research into JFK's assassination has given way, has lost ground to, a highly speculative form of inquiry which has one "feeling more and thinking less." Playing to the emotions, rather than to a balance of reason and emotion, tenuous relationships and far-fetched theory have become the foundation for truth, supplanting facts, common sense and reason. America! Don't park your mind while your heart is running! Ask your questions, but think about the answers you receive. What we need to do is to go back and re-examine the basic points of contention in this case and be willing, as we investigate, to accept with our hearts what our brains tell us is truth.

As you read this book, I believe you will be challenged, as I have been, to think anew about the places, people and events of November 22, 1963 and to have your opinions altered by Jim Moore's insightful research and writing.

Carpe Diem. "Seize the day!" Upon reading Jim's manuscript, I was struck by the calm, lucid manner in which he skillfully unravels what has become an emotional Gordian knot—the assassination of President Kennedy. Nothing has so frustrated me as a researcher, over the last three to five years as the unprofessional manner in which certain individuals have tarnished the image of legitimate investigation into the late president's assassination. By holding bi-monthly "we've solved it" media events, some have hyped wild claims which are made without a hint of concrete evidence to support one single assertion. Meanwhile, competent, serious inquiry is either brushed aside or ignored because it lacks sensational elements or because it runs contrary to the deeply held beliefs of others. The situation is reminiscent of earlier days when the government had similar reactions to researchers who challenged an official train of thought with a "but" or "what about . . . ." The pendulum swings.

It must be that to finally solve the case and answer the question as to what actually happened on that tragic day in November, 1963, we need the thoughtful, meticulous type of investigation offered through the efforts of researchers such as Jim Moore. If we are to know the truth, we must be willing to consider those facts which upon first inspection, we would mentally toss aside because we cannot or will not accept the logical conclusions to which they lead.

To be honest, Jim and I differ on a few points, but as a friend and colleague (and having worked together on the Sixth Floor Exhibit), I value Jim's honest, open, probing type of investigation which forces me to honestly evaluate my own beliefs and prevents me from holding on, too tightly, to untenable positions.

I believe that as the years progress, we will find that what we had been looking for all along was within our grasp from the beginning and that researchers such as Jim Moore were the still, calm voices of reason in an age of sensational, accusatory screams.

Carl Alan Henry
August 28, 1990

Contents

I

View from the Sixth Floor

THROUGH THE HALF-OPENED WINDOW CREPT THE SOUNDS OF THE CITY. Below were buses moving toward the expressways, carrying their human cargo to darker, more remote parts of town. The hooves of horses slapped lazily against the unremitting concrete, as the tourists rode through the streets in horse-drawn carriages. Once in awhile, I would stare out the window and gaze after them, only to be totally disarmed when they turned to stare back at me. I was, quite literally, the last thing they expected to see.

I was standing in the most famous window in the world—the sixth-floor southeast corner window of the old Texas School Book Depository. Here, more than a quarter-century earlier, Lee Harvey Oswald had fired the shots that killed President John F. Kennedy and plunged the entire globe into mourning.

Tonight, in the eerie stillness of the old building, I was bringing that dark day back to life. Scattered around me on the ancient board floor were copies of official photographs that detailed the arrangement of the hundreds of boxes of books that the assassin had used to shield himself from view. With single-minded precision, I fabricated each box, then placed it into position according to the photos. The corner window was being reborn.

Most writers of assassination lore had given the impression that the book boxes were haphazardly scattered about with no particular form or purpose. As I finished placing the cartons nearest the window and moved to the stacks of boxes further out on the floor, I saw that the descriptions I read had misled me.

Re-creating the stacks of boxes behind the shield of cartons around the window, my mind drifted back a score of years, to my first fascination with the assassination . . . and the beginning of my odyssey.

I WAS ONLY EIGHT YEARS OLD WHEN I CAUGHT THE "DISEASE."* Struggling through the lofty prose of William Manchester's *Death of a President* and then through the morass of inaccuracies that make up Jim Bishop's *The Day Kennedy Was Shot*, I found myself left with nothing but uncertainty. In my own childish way, I could not explain the vague feelings of uneasiness growing within me. Years later, veteran assassination researcher Harold Weisberg would remark that my analysis of the pair of books was "a display of maturity of which most adults were not capable".[1]

Those vague uncertainties continued to abide within me for years. In my junior-high and high-school days, it wasn't uncommon for a teacher or classmate to express the opinion that I was playing with a few cards missing from my proverbial deck. Their suspicions were probably confirmed when, in the summer of 1976, *The Arkansas Democrat* newspaper asked its readers, "What kind of nut is this?" Fortunately for me, few of them really cared.**

DARKNESS HAD FALLEN. The fans and air-conditioning system on the sixth floor were turned off since I was working alone there. Inside the glass enclosure that would protect the corner window from the ravages of tourism the temperature climbed higher and higher. I had opened the window to catch a bit of the cool February night air, but that wasn't enough. Grimy and perspiring, I set yet another carton into place and turned back to the window to rest for a moment. Sitting down on the old window sill, I raised the window as high as I could and looked down, across Dealey Plaza.

MY FIRST TRIP TO DALLAS WITH MY PARENTS in the late 1960s happened before I'd done much reading on the assassination. Dealey Plaza, the rectangle of land downtown where the President was killed, was a confusing place for anyone who didn't know what he was looking for. There were no markers to guide me on that first visit. I walked away with only a vague impression of the hallowed ground I was supposed

---

* *The "disease" is a term given by* Six Seconds in Dallas *author Josiah Thompson to the obsession that grips those who actively research this case.*

** *July 26, 1976 issue, page 1.*

to have seen and touched.

Five years later, after I had begun reading everything I could find on the assassination, I pestered my father until he agreed to drive me back to Dallas from our rural Arkansas home. The half-day trek culminated in my wandering up and down Elm Street where the President was killed, taking Polaroid photos of the scene, and longing in vain to find my way inside the long-since deserted Book Depository.

I TOOK A LONG, AUDIBLE BREATH. Anyone listening on the still sixth floor might have heard me sigh. I watched an old man on the sidewalk staring back up at me—just as I had done, years before.

I SPENT MORE TIME IN THE PLAZA enduring the scorching summer of 1974. Two weeks vacationing in Dallas allowed me to talk with dozens of witnesses, walk through the assassination site again and again, and look for the one stroke of luck that would, for me, break the case wide open.

Obviously, that stroke of luck never came.

Actually, I was plowing some novel ground for a researcher—setting aside for the moment the fact that I was only 15 years old. Many of the critics and researchers I had corresponded with had spent only a few days in Dallas. Some had dashed back home to write books on the assassination. And incredibly enough, I was later to discover that some best-selling authors had never bothered to come to Dallas at all.

MY MEMORIES WERE ONCE AGAIN INTERRUPTED.

On Elm Street, below and to my right, a car slowed to a stop in the middle lane, near the spot where life ended and eternity began for John F. Kennedy. Considering the traffic that night, I thought that the driver either wasn't very bright or didn't care if someone struck his car from behind. Quickly, I mentally measured the distance from my window sill vantage point down to the auto's back seat. It still wasn't all that far.

UNTIL I WAS TEN OR SO, I had assumed that Oswald had probably acted alone and that there was nothing behind the rumors of a conspiracy. My desire to believe what the government told me had been enhanced by the fact that, in the small town where I lived, there was no library. The libraries in the larger villages some twenty miles away considered themselves lucky to have a copy of the *Warren Report*—the *Report of the President's Commission on the Assassination of President Kennedy* among their holdings.

My confidence in the government report would be shaken when I ordered a copy of Mark Lane's *Rush to Judgment,* the first really successful book attacking the Report and its conclusions. I can still remember that I ordered the book from a Publisher's Clearinghouse catalog and that it cost me the incredible sum of a dollar. It also changed my life.

Rush to Judgment was four or five years old by the time I acquired my copy. As I ripped it from the package at the post office and carried it with me to school, I had no idea what Lane would say or how convincingly he would write. I recall that I had to pry myself away from chapters like "The Gauze Curtain" and "The Magic Bullet" to pay attention in class.

Pointedly, Lane's book was not all that good. Lane's research had actually been done for him by a small army of amateur sleuths. In my haste to finish the book, I raced through the final chapter and past an all-important paragraph: "It may be asked why I have accepted some testimony that detracts from the Commission's case while rejecting other testimony or parts of testimony that support the case . . . ."[2]

In a word, Lane wasn't telling the whole story. But, I had discovered, neither was the Warren Commission. Nonetheless, *Rush to Judgment* was a turning point in my life. From the moment I put the book down, I took nothing else for granted. Convinced that conspirators of some sort had plotted and carried out the assassination of President Kennedy, I began my odyssey—my quest for the truth.

THOUGHTS HAD INVADED my feverish reconstruction of the sixth floor scene. The night was burning down like a fuse. It was already eight o'clock, and I had to finish my work. I mentally pictured my wife waiting in our Irving, Texas home—and wondering why I wasn't there with her.

It was hard to get the stacks of boxes to fit exactly the arrangement depicted in the photos I was using for reference. The most tedious part of the project—moving stacks of cartons around until they matched the source material—had only begun.*

OBSESSION FOR DETAIL had characterized my odyssey. It had taken me through letter battles with leading critics and researchers, past careful study of the autopsy notes, diagrams, and photos, and through analysis of bullet flight paths through the President and Texas Governor John Connally, who had been sitting in front of Kennedy and was himself seriously wounded. I once asked a classmate to sit in a most peculiar pose while I measured the angle of declination of an imaginary bullet path through his body.

Without even a projector to show it, I scraped together funds to purchase the Zapruder film. The Z-film, as we all called it back then, was the only motion picture of the assassination taken from the President's side of the limousine. It demonstrated in gripping detail and clarity the sequence of shots and their effects on Kennedy and Connally. If Dealey Plaza had become something of a religious ground for me, then owning the Zapruder film was like possessing a relic of the true cross.

I sent Midlothian, Texas, researcher Penn Jones, Jr., author of a series of books called *Forgive My Grief*, $15 in hard-earned cash for my super-eight-millimeter Z-film. When it arrived, my long-suffering father drove his car to the next little town and borrowed a projector from a friend. Late that evening, over and over again, President Kennedy "came back to life" and "died" a silent, shattering death, all on my parents' living room wall.**

It wasn't long before I was taking the Z-film on the road, showing it to anyone who would sit still for eighteen seconds. In early 1976, after it had been shown on national television, I stole the show from my high

---

*Another issue is which depiction is most accurate. Newsmen and law enforcement officials moved boxes after the "sniper's nest" was discovered, resulting in different arrangements in different photos. I was conviced that the photos taken by newspaper photographer Jack Beers were most correct. I relied on them—and on photos taken from the street at the time of the assassination—as primary source material.

**Tom Miller, in his Assassination Please Almanac, notes "an absolutely eerie sensation when the Zapruder film is rewound, showing the dead President coming alive once again, history reversed by an eight-millimeter projector."

school's Bicentennial Fair by being unpatriotic enough to show the film and give a brief lecture on the conspiracy that robbed us of our President.

The House Select Committee on Assassinations was created in the fall of that same year. The event brought rejoicing to critics and researchers like myself. Here, finally, was our golden opportunity to prove to the world that we weren't really paranoid crazies after all.

The HSCA went through the ground we'd plowed, and through a lot of ground that should never have been plowed at all. Panelists looked at disappearing assassins in the bushes, listened to Dictabelt tapes, and studied bullet trajectories with a grim sense of purpose. They took more than two years to issue a report that most critics labeled another whitewash. Despite my sensitivity to the case, I began to wonder whether any government-sponsored investigation would ever satisfy people like Lane, Weisberg and their colleagues.

Plainly, the HSCA findings were flawed, but to a minor degree. On the whole, I was pleased with their effort. For the next ten years, I contented myself with doing an occasional slide show, reading new books on the case, and keeping my lines of communication open with other researchers. But slowly and gradually, I ceased to be one of "them" any longer. I didn't fit in with the critics.

THAT PROCESS OF LEARNING TO THINK FOR MYSELF, I believe, was what had brought me once again to the old sixth floor. This bit of manual labor, moving book cartons around, was a part of my contribution to President Kennedy and the truth. I was trying to do something positive for the memory of a nation.

I pushed another stack of cartons a few inches to the right, then walked out of the glass enclosure to study the results. With nearly all the boxes in place, I could better judge the faithfulness of my re-creation efforts. To say that the results surprised me would be a vast understatement.

I was seeing the corner window in all its deadly glory for the first time since investigators walked away from the crime scene a quarter of a century earlier. Not even the members of the Warren Commission or the House Select Committee had seen the stacks of boxes in their original positions. Two motion pictures based on the assassination, *Executive Action* and *The Trial of Lee Harvey Oswald*, had shown audiences a care-less re-creation in another building, or an empty, barn-like sixth floor.

I felt like I was intruding on history.

Staring wide-eyed at the arrangement of book cartons, I knew that whoever had positioned them had done so with considerable care. The boxes had been stacked so as to obscure the assassin from every angle within the building and outside. This had been premeditated murder.

It was at that moment that I felt the last of my vague uncertainties drain away. Actually, I had solved the assassination for myself some months before, a solution detailed later in this book. But until tonight, I lacked the one thing that turns belief into a crusade: I lacked the conviction that I was right. That sense of purpose was provided by something I had created . . . not from some new piece of evidence I had found. The calm assurance came from the re-creation of the corner window on the sixth floor. That night marked the high point of my personal odyssey.

BEFORE TAKING A LOOK AT THE INVESTIGATIONS of President Kennedy's assassination and at the criticism of those inquiries, a brief review of the facts surrounding the crime is in order. Those of you who consider yourselves well-versed in assassination lore might wish to skip ahead to the next chapter.

In November 1963, President Kennedy and his advisors planned a two-day, five-city tour of Texas. The purpose of the trip was to boost the President's chances for re-election. No Democrat had ever been elected President without Texas' electoral votes in his column. Kennedy also wanted to heal a rift in the state's Democratic party leadership. Some advisors had warned the President not to travel to Dallas, where his United Nations ambassador, Adlai Stevenson, had been struck with a protest sign some weeks before. Nonetheless, the Dallas trip became a part of the Presidential agenda.

Secret Service agents, Winston Lawson and Forrest Sorrels, decided on the route for the 45-minute Presidential motorcade. President Kennedy was to speak at a luncheon to be held in the Dallas Trade Mart, along the city's Stemmons Freeway.

The motorcade route was published in the Dallas newspapers beginning on November 19. The President was due to arrive in Dallas on November 22. Advance publication of the motorcade route made it clear that the Presidential parade would proceed west along Dallas' Main Street, enter Dealey Plaza at the end of the downtown area by turning north for a block onto Houston Street, then back southwest onto Elm Street for the final sprint onto Stemmons and toward the Trade Mart.

Standing at the northwest corner of Elm and Houston streets is an old, orange-brick, seven-story building. It had been built in 1901 as offices for the Southern Rock Island Plow Company. In 1963, it housed another tenant—the Texas School Book Depository.

The Depository was a firm engaged in the distribution of school textbooks. One of the newest clerks there—hired on October 15—was a young ex-Marine named Lee Harvey Oswald.

The 24-year-old Oswald had a checkered past. In September of 1959, he received a hardship discharge from the Marines and then defected to the Soviet Union. Russian officials, unsure of the young man, settled him in the city of Minsk, where he worked in a radio factory. He met and married a young Russian pharmacist, Marina Prusakova.

In the fall of 1962, the Oswald couple and an infant daughter returned to the United States with the help of a loan from the State Department. Living in New Orleans during the late spring and summer of 1963, Oswald drifted in and out of work, attracted media attention by handing out pro-Castro leaflets to passersby, and plotted to gain entrance to communist Cuba. After a late September trip to Mexico City failed to achieve this purpose, Oswald came to Dallas to join his wife and child. Marina and the baby were living in the Irving, Texas home of Ruth and Michael Paine, a couple who had befriended the Oswalds earlier that year.

Among his possessions, Oswald brought with him a 1940-vintage Italian army rifle. The 6.5 millimeter Mannlicher-Carcano had been ordered by mail in late March 1963. Oswald bought the rifle with a four-power scope attached. Establishing himself in a Dallas boarding house,

Oswald commuted to Irving with a co-worker nearly every weekend. Unexpectedly, Oswald arrived at the Paine residence on Thursday afternoon, November 21. He told his co-worker, young Wes Frazier, that he needed to pick up some curtain rods to take back to his furnished room.

What transpired that night between Oswald and his wife is still a matter of controversy. William Manchester asserts that, sometime during the evening, Oswald went "mad."[4] Whatever the events of that Thursday evening, Oswald rode back to Dallas with Frazier the next morning carrying a long and bulky package, presumably the disassembled Mannlicher-Carcano rifle.[5*]

At 12:30 p.m. November 22, shots rang out in Dealey Plaza as the Presidential motorcade traveled down Elm Street. A bullet hit Kennedy in the right shoulder and penetrated his throat. Governor Connally was struck in the back. The bullet blew apart his fifth rib, smashed through his wrist and embedded itself in his thigh. Finally, a bullet hit the back of the President's head and blew out the right front of his skull.

Doctors at nearby Parkland Hospital tried to revive the stricken President, but the damage had been done. Kennedy was pronounced dead at 1:00 p.m. Governor Connally eventually recovered from his wounds.

Meanwhile, back in Dealey Plaza, the search was on for the gunman. A witness, Howard Brennan, told police that he had seen a young white male firing a rifle from a corner window of the Book Depository's sixth floor. By the time Brennan had given his description to authorities, police officers were attempting to seal off the building. The Depository superintendent, Roy Truly, couldn't account for several employees. One of them was Lee Oswald.

Just after 1:15 p.m., Dallas police converged on the Oak Cliff section of the city, some minutes southwest of the downtown area. There Officer J.D. Tippit had been shot to death by a pedestrian armed with a .38-caliber revolver. At 1:45 p.m., police arrested a young man in the Texas Theater, a few blocks from the Tippit killing site. Armed with a revolver, the suspect jumped up as officers approached. He shouted

---

* Time *magazine's Ed Magnuson wrote me in 1977: "You really think he was carrying curtain rods to work that day?"*

"This is it!" and tried to shoot a policeman. He was subdued, taken to police headquarters downtown for questioning and held for investigation in the murder of Officer Tippit. His name was Lee Harvey Oswald.

As the world mourned President Kennedy, the case against Oswald in the murders of the Chief Executive and Officer Tippit began to come together. The Mannlicher-Carcano rifle was found on the sixth floor, hidden between stacks of book boxes.* Three spent rifle shells were discovered near the southeast corner window, along with a handmade bag of brown wrapping paper and tape.

The shells were traced to the rifle and the rifle to Oswald. The shells cast aside by Officer Tippit's killer as the assailant ran through the Oak Cliff neighborhood were proven to have been fired in the revolver Oswald possessed when he was arrested. Police Captain Will Fritz and a host of law enforcement officials questioned Oswald for two days, without taking notes or tape recording the interrogations. The young man maintained his innocence in both murders.

On Sunday, November 24, Oswald was being transferred from the city jail to the county facility at Dealey Plaza when he was shot by Dallas nightclub owner Jack Ruby. Clumsily, officers tried to revive Oswald with artificial respiration while they waited for an ambulance to arrive. The accused assassin was rushed to Parkland Hospital, where President Kennedy had died two days earlier. Oswald was pronounced dead at 1:07 p.m. on Sunday.

---

* *Dallas box manufacturer Rick Lane and I also re-created the boxes near the corner staircase, where police discovered Oswald's rifle. As a result of our work there, I am convinced that Oswald had prepared the site early on the morning of the assassination. A second-tier row of boxes had been pushed forward to create an overhang so that the rifle could be easily and hurriedly hidden underneath. After dropping the Carcano, Oswald walked four steps to his right and proceeded down the stairwall. The corner staircase was diagonally across the room from the southeast corner window.*

1. Letter to the author, March 18, 1975.
2. Mark Lane, *Rush to Judgment*, (Holt, Rinehart & Winston, 1966), 338.
3. Tom Miller, *Assassination Please Almanac*, (Henry Regency Co. 1977), 35.
4. William Manchester, *Death of a President*, (Harper & Row, 1967), 104.
5. Report of the President's Commission on the Assassination of President Kennedy, (Bantam Books Edition, 1964), 125.

Hereafter, all citations from the Report are listed as "WCR," followed by the page number. Citations referring to the 26 volumes of hearings and exhibit subsequently issued by the Warren Commission are listed thus "7H, 100"—meaning volume 7, page 100.

II

The Blue Ribbon Inquiry

JUST FOUR DAYS AFTER THE ASSASSINATION OF PRESIDENT KENNEDY, the Communist party newspaper, *The Worker*, called for an investigation of the killing and suggested that the inquest be headed by Chief Justice Earl Warren.

Three days later, President Johnson appointed a seven-member "blue ribbon" panel to look into the assassination and to report its findings. Members included Rep. Gerald Ford (R-Mich.), Sen. Richard Russell (D-Ga.), Rep. Hale Boggs (D-Ala.), John McCloy, former president of the World Bank, Sen. John Sherman Cooper (R-Ky.) and Allen Dulles, former Central Intelligence Agency Director.

Despite Earl Warren's reluctance to serve, the President appointed him chairman.

I like to think of Johnson's actions as mere coincidence. Other critics and researchers, however, haven't been as kind. Still, I seriously doubt that the new President had taken the time to read *The Worker* and decided to act upon its recommendations.

Truth to tell, Johnson actually appointed the Commission in part to head off another inquiry—this one proposed by the Attorney General of the State of Texas.

Waggoner Carr announced on November 25, the day President Kennedy was buried, that a court of inquiry would be held in the Lone Star State "to develop fully and disclose openly"[1] the circumstances surrounding the assassination. First, the Federal Bureau of Investigation was to conduct its own study and give its findings to the President; the Texas court would then hold public hearings to talk with eyewitnesses. Then, as a final step, a Presidential Commission would evaluate the facts and reach conclusions, which would be passed onto President

Lyndon Johnson.

The next day, U.S. Sen. Everett Dirksen asked in his dulcet tones that the Senate Judiciary Committee conduct its own inquiry into the assassination.[2] His suggestion received a considerable amount of support from a bipartisan selection of Senators. Congressman Charles Goodell made a similar proposal in the House a day later.

And so, on November 29, "to avoid parallel investigations and to concentrate fact-finding in a body having the broadest national mandate,"[3] President Johnson appointed the Commission and asked it to "ascertain, evaluate, and report on" the facts of the assassination and the murder of Lee Oswald. Almost from the day of its creation, the panel was referred to as "The Warren Commission" by those who followed the assassination story.*

Today, we can't imagine having no Warren Commission upon which to pin the judgment of history. Johnson would have liked to have dispensed with the assassination investigation upon receipt of the FBI report. Thank goodness that he decided not to stop there–history and several critics' bank accounts would be infinitely poorer.

The Warren Commission met formally for the first time only thirteen days after the assassination. Earl Warren presided over the gathering of august and influential men who, as Allen Dulles pointed out, "had a lifetime's experience in dealing with extraordinary problems, and . . . knew what had to be done."[4]

Thus, the decisive Commission quickly disposed of any thought of letting the FBI report form the entire investigative portion of its work. The Commission, decided the panel members, would hold its own investigation . . . at least, as long as they could hire someone to do it for them.

With great rapidity, the Commission agreed to hire J. Lee Rankin, a former Solicitor General for the United States, as General Counsel. The Warren Commission investigation thus became a task like any other—contracted and paid for.

The last action taken by Commissioners at that first meeting was to ask Texas Attorney General Waggoner Carr to postpone his state's

---

* *Playwright Barb Garson, in her stage production* MacBird! *has the "Earl of Warren" commenting "Oh, whine and pout, that ever I was born to bury doubt."*

Court of Inquiry until the Commission had finished its work. Warren noted that conducting investigations simultaneously might lead the American public to mistaken conclusions and that the inquiries might step on each other's toes. Finally, the chairman brought to mind the thought of Jack Ruby, who had killed Lee Oswald on November 24. Surely Carr wouldn't want to risk prejudicial publicity which would affect Ruby's trial, would he? One can almost hear Warren answering his own question.

J. Lee Rankin's task was simple enough—become the Commission's "executive director" and organize the investigation. So, Rankin not only worked for the Commission, he was the panel's middleman, acting as a liaison between the Commission and other government agencies, as well as between the Commissioners and their staff.

The FBI's Summary Report on the assassination arrived in Commission offices on December 9.[5] There the four blue-bound volumes reposed until the next panel meeting a week later. The December 16 gathering was a fateful one—Commissioners decided to rely on governmental investigative agencies for field work. Unfortunately, this meant that the FBI, CIA and Secret Service would be allowed to investigate themselves.*

The Commission decided to withhold judgment, interpreted as approval by some critics, of the FBI Summary Report. They gave Rankin the authority to put together a staff and make an examination of the thousands of documents the FBI relied upon. Thus would the unresolved questions or issues be ferreted out for Commission review.

The '63 holiday season and the first ten days of the new year were critical times for the Commission as it put together its investigative agenda. Department of Justice liaison Howard Willens deserves credit for organizing the process; he suggested a five-area investigation concept, with a junior and senior staff lawyer assigned to each area. The theory was that the pair of attorneys could resolve any minor problems they encountered.

Obviously, Commissioners were hopeful that they would only be called upon to deal with major difficulties that the staff could not resolve.[6]

---

* Thus, we didn't hear of Lee Oswald threatening to blow up Dallas FBI headquarters until 1975.

Each team would write a chapter on its findings, and the chapters would be put together to form the final report. Area One delved into basic facts surrounding the assassination. Area Two sought to identify the assassin. Area Three discussed Oswald's background, and—assuming the result of Area Two was to identify him as the killer—discussed his possible motive. Area Four probed the question of conspiracy. The Fifth Area dealt with the killing of Oswald by Jack Ruby.

Trouble came to the Commission almost immediately. January 22, Texas Attorney General Carr told Rankin about an allegation that Oswald had been an informant on the FBI payroll. When Rankin told Warren of the charge, the Chief Justice called an emergency Commission session. That afternoon members decided to ask both Carr and Dallas District Attorney Henry Wade to come to Washington. Both men arrived in the Capital two days later.[7] From the Texans, the Commission learned that neither man knew from whence the Oswald-FBI story had come, or whether it was true or false. Three days later the panel decided to inform the FBI of the charge and to examine the relationship Oswald had with government agencies.

Meanwhile, difficulty abounded on the staff's side of the inquiry. The problem arose when attorneys carefully analyzed the Zapruder film of the assassination. From the reactions of Kennedy and Connally, it became obvious that the shots fired at the motorcade were not, as had been originally thought, even in timing. Staffers concurred with FBI and Secret Service representatives in noting that Kennedy and Connally appeared to have been hit only a second or so apart—too fast for Oswald to have fired his bolt-action rifle twice.*

Mired in quicksand with these two difficulties, the Commission began its work in earnest on February 3. Rankin questioned Marina Oswald for four days about her dead husband. Her answers left the staff with dozens of uncertainties. During the staff meeting that followed, one of the staff attorneys threatened to resign unless Mrs. Oswald was brought back to Washington for additional questioning. Rankin ended the discussion by saying that the Commission was prepared to believe

---

* This "problem" gave rise to the famous single-bullet theory—one bullet hitting both Kennedy and Connally.

Marina's testimony.

Then, late that month, the Commission asked American Bar Association President, Walter Craig, to monitor hearings and assure that they did "conform to the basic principles of American justice."[8] Judging from the record, Craig's participation in Commission hearings reflects no doubt on his part that the panel was acting fairly and equitably.

The Commissioners themselves—the seven atop the mount, so to speak—were not in touch with the staff's day-to-day investigation. Junior Counsel Wesley Liebeler was asked what the Commissioners actually did, and he replied, "Nothing."[9] Simply, the Commissioners directed the course of their inquiry, while the staff did the investigating, interviewed witnesses, solved problems, and ultimately wrote the report.

Jacqueline Kennedy testified at her home on June 5. Chief Justice Warren and Commissioner Ford headed to Dallas on June 7 to talk with Jack Ruby. Ford later wrote that "Ruby was an unstable person and although willing to talk, he spoke in a rambling fashion and didn't contribute much."[10]

The Commission announced an end to the hearings on June 17. For the next three months, staff members argued, wrote, then rewrote chapters of the report. When galley proofs were presented to staffers on September 4, Wes Liebeler wrote a 26-page memo attacking the section of the report dealing with the identity of the assassin. That portion had to be rewritten.

Finally, on September 24, the Report was submitted to President Johnson. He accepted the thick volume from the Chief Justice with the comment, "It's very heavy."[11]

And four days later, the Report was made public. The Commission's work—for all practical purposes—was finished.*

The Warren Report was embraced by a nation eager for answers. With the publication of the Report and later, of the twenty-six volumes

---

* *Nearly three years after the assassination—November 4, 1966—President Johnson told a press conference that if evidence were discovered that warranted the panel's attention, the Commission "would take action." The Commission was non-existent after the Report was submitted to the President more than two years before. Johnson said he knew of no evidence that would cast doubt on the Report's conclusions.*

of supporting evidence and testimony, President Johnson was rid of the assassination as a political millstone. The country, in a word, could return to normal.

But the critics made sure the normalcy didn't last long.

Since they bear so heavily on future chapters, it is wise for us to pause for a moment and reflect on the conclusions reached by the Warren Commission:

1. *The shots which killed President Kennedy and wounded Governor Connally were fired from the sixth floor window at the southeast corner of the Texas School Book Depository.*

2. *The weight of the evidence indicates that there were three shots fired.*

3. *Although it is not necessary to any essential findings of the Commission to determine just which shot hit Governor Connally, there is very persuasive evidence from the experts to indicate that the same bullet which pierced thePresident's throat also caused GovernorConnally's wounds. Governor Connally's testimony and certain other factors have given rise to some difference of opinion as to this probability. There is no question in the mind of any member of the Commission, however, that all the shots which caused the President's and Governor Connally's wounds were fired from the sixth floor window of the Texas School Book Depository.*

4. *The shots which killed President Kennedy and wounded Governor Connally were fired by Lee Harvey Oswald.*

5. *Oswald killed Dallas Police patrolman J.D.Tippit approximately 45 minutes after the assassination.*

6. *Within 80 minutes of the assassination and 35 minutes of the Tippit killing, Oswald resisted arrest at the theater by attempting to shoot another Dallas police officer.*

Further, the Commission concluded that Oswald was treated fairly by the Dallas police, unfairly by the press, and that neither he nor Jack Ruby were engaged in a conspiracy to murder the President. The Report also stated that the Secret Service might have heightened its methods of operation in an effort to afford Kennedy greater protection against threats to his life.*

---

* When Lyndon Johnson visited Dallas the next year, he rode in the same limousine Kennedy used—but with the bullet-proof bubbletop in place.

The storm of criticism began to break soon after the Commission released its Report. This is due in part to how the critics (and the public) perceived the Commission arriving at its conclusions. The consensus has always been that the Commission began with the conviction that Oswald was the lone gunman, and then proceeded to develop evidence to fit its pre-determined answer. Unfortunately, this sort of biased inquiry led to the avoidance of many key and controversial questions, the stringent cross-examination of witnesses, and a tendency to overstate the importance of supporting evidence.

Notwithstanding how the panel arrived at its conclusions, it's my belief that the Commission reached the only conclusions tenable to reasonable men. Even without their self-imposed "mental block" against possible conspiracy, I believe that the staff would eventually have arrived at the same answer—that Oswald, acting alone, killed the President. All the available evidence, when viewed as a whole, pointed in that direction. But—and this is a crucial exception—had the Commission explored every other avenue, the probe would have taken much longer. Staffers were fighting for time, and President Johnson was anxious to receive the full report. Who knows how long a really proper investigation might have taken?

I've already mentioned the problem the Commission courted by allowing its investigative agencies—the FBI, CIA, and the Secret Service—to investigate themselves. The panel also did itself irreparable harm by not viewing the Kennedy autopsy x-rays and photographs. Like some modern-day critics, the Commissioners might not have known how to read x-rays, but they could have forestalled later charges that they neglected this evidence intentionally.*

---

* When I first saw a bootleg copy of an autopsy photo some years ago, I was nauseated. Now, they're featured as "evidence" in some paperback books on the assassination.

1. Edward J. Epstein, E, (Viking Press, 1966), 20.
2 Ibid.
3. Ibid.
4. Ibid., 21.
5. Ibid., 23.
6. Ibid., 22.
7. Ibid., 31.
8. Lane, 321.
9. Epstein, 39*.
10. Gerald R. Ford, *A Time to Heal* (Harper & Row, 1979), 75.
11. Miller, iv.

Liebler says he never made this statement. Others quoted by Epstein have voiced similar complaints. See Chapter Six for a detailed explanation.

III

The Assassin
Who Never Was

I CAN SAY WITHOUT RESERVATION that I've spent more time in Dealey Plaza, the site of the assassination, than any other critic or researcher who has ever written about this case. The Plaza itself is unique in geography. It's also a vast echo chamber capable of multiplying sounds such as the retorts from the rifle shots that killed President Kennedy. Critics who ignore this fact and rely on witness testimony of shots "heard" from the grassy knoll or triple underpass are really misleading their readers.

Later in this book we'll see that all the shots which hit President Kennedy and Governor Connally were fired from behind and above them. The facts fail to support the belief by some critics that the President's wounds were caused by shots from the front.*

Dealey Plaza is a rectangular plot of land split down the middle by Dallas' Main Street. Commerce Street forms the south side of the plaza as the roadway curves eastward from an underpass. Elm Street, the stretch of pavement on which Kennedy died, curves down to meet Commerce and Main. Elm forms the northern border of the Plaza.

Along both the south side of Commerce and the north side of Elm Street lie elevated grass-covered rises jutting some 25 feet above the roadway. These small hills are crowned by pavilions built by the WPA during the Depression. Adjacent to these concrete structures are parking lots, bordered on the Elm Street knoll by a wooden picket fence.

The Presidential limousine was directly in front of the white concrete pavilion when the fatal shot was fired.

---

* High Treason *author Robert Groden claims a frontal hit by dismissing the autopsy photos and x-rays as forgeries.*

In a word, eyewitnesses standing nearer the Book Depository generally thought that the shots came from within or close to the building, while those standing nearer the knoll or the underpass were convinced that the shots had been fired near their position. The knoll seems to attract the suspicion of critics. In *Accessories After the Fact* the late Sylvia Meagher wrote: "Certainly there were numerous reasons for believing that shots had come from the grassy knoll . . . on it there are trees and bushes, a fence, concrete monuments, and colonnades, all offering a place of concealment and a clear line of fire."[1] Ms. Meagher ignored the fact that the Plaza is ringed with tall buildings which offered better accommodations for would-be assassins. *Accessories After the Fact* goes on to add that testimony demonstrated that many witnesses believed shots came from the knoll. Others saw a puff of smoke rising from the bushes there, and a few saw a man running from the scene.[2]

The fleeing man Ms. Meagher mentioned also cropped up in Mark Lane's *Rush to Judgment*. Lane mentions an affidavit given to Dallas County Sheriff's Deputies by one Jesse Price, who witnessed the assassination from atop the roof of the Terminal Annex Building, located directly across from the Depository but some three city blocks removed.

Lane interviewed Price atop the same roof vantage point in the spring of 1966. Price described the man he saw running, then added that: "He was bare headed, and he was running very fast, which gave me the suspicion that he was doing the shooting, but I could be mistaken."[3] Lane mentions that Price added information that the man "was carrying something in his right hand, (which) could have been a gun."[4]

I did talk with Mr. Price's widow during a trip to Dallas in the summer of 1974. She told me that she wished her husband was still alive to talk with me, saying that Mr. Price "loved to tell that story to people."

In *Rush to Judgment*, Lane asked Price where he saw the man running. Price replied that the man he saw fled "over behind that wooden fence past the cars and over behind the Texas Depository Building."[5] What Lane doesn't mention is that for the man Price saw to run behind the wooden fence, he would of necessity have begun his flight in front of it, and in plain view of the witnesses who lined the south side of Elm Street. Included in the hardback and paperback editions of

Lane's book is a rudimentary diagram of Dealey Plaza, incapable of providing the reader with enough information to make this determination for himself. The Plaza photo that adorns the hardback dust jacket is over-exposed and sufficiently distant as to be equally worthless.

Most likely, the man Price saw running was an eyewitness who had just been scared out of his wits by what he saw. Panic-stricken witnesses running in fright are visible in the Nix and Muchmore films of the assassination.[6]

Another eyewitness, Jean L. Hill, has been telling researchers for years that she witnessed a man running behind the knoll. The latest additions to her story are a "flash of light" and a "puff of smoke" from atop the knoll as well.[7]

A reporter from the *Dallas Times Herald* apparently tried to convince Mrs. Hill that she could not have seen a gunman running behind the knoll because she had no way to view the area from her south Elm Street vantage point (unless she had witnessed the assassination from a helicopter). When Commission counsel interviewed Mrs. Hill, the witness became uncertain if the reporter was who he said he was. Mrs. Hill seemed to think that she might have actually been talking with a Secret Service or FBI agent. Ms. Meagher, who, incredibly enough, believed Oswald totally innocent in the assassination,[8] included the Jean Hill incident in her book as additional evidence of an assassination cover-up perpetuated by government agents. Kinder readers will note that the confusion seems to be in the mind of Mrs. Hill.

Standing where Mrs. Hill stood on November 22, you can't see behind the rise that culminates at the top of the knoll. It's impossible to see anyone running, walking, or standing behind the wooden fence, and you certainly can't observe anyone running toward the point where railroad tracks in the area join the triple underpass. Yet, Mrs. Hill testified that she had.[9] Writer Anthony Summers in his book, *Conspiracy*, tries to get around the physical impossibility of Mrs. Hill's observations by putting her across Elm Street in time to see the mythical gunman make his sprint to freedom. He writes: "Hill had run impetuously across the road, dodging between cars while the motorcade was still going by. She was ahead of the field in the parking lot . . . ."[10] This is absurd. Spectator Wilma Bond took a series of still photos from her vantage point behind and east of Mrs. Hill. In one photo, clearly taken several moments after the assassination, spectators are indeed rushing up the grassy slope, still trying to determine the source of the mysterious shots. Mrs. Hill, clearly visible in a red raincoat, is still sitting on the ground on the south side of Elm, alongside her friend, Mary Moorman.[11]

Based on her eyewitness experience, Mrs. Hill has opened her own research center to delve into the controversy surrounding the assassination—a fair bit of which she has helped to create. Her rather unique business card touts her as the "closest witness" to the President at the time of the fatal shot.[12]

I had thought that the dead President's wife, Governor and Mrs. Connally, and Secret Service agents Kellerman and Greer (all of whom were called as witnesses by the Warren Commission) would have been closest to Mr. Kennedy, based on the fact that all five occupied the limousine with him. Perhaps Mrs. Hill has more recent information.

Whatever Mrs. Hill saw on November 22, it could scarcely have been another assassin. Such a gunman, if he had existed, would surely have been long gone from the scene by the time Mrs. Hill finally made it to the top of the grassy knoll.

In her testimony before the Warren Commission, Mrs. Hill stated that she "ran across the street to see the man" she saw running from the scene. She claims she was stopped at the top of the rise by a tall, slender man who identified himself as a Secret Service agent.[13] Mrs. Hill says the "man" blocked her view of the running man and kept her from pursuing him. An alleged Secret Service Agent was also encountered on the knoll by three law enforcement officers: Deputy Constable Seymour Weitzman, Sergeant D. V. Harkness, and Patrolman J. M. Smith.[14] Since all Secret Service agents were still with the motorcade at the time of this encounter, it's apparent that the individual on the knoll was, at the least, displaying bogus credentials.

I do not know who this man really was, or what he was doing atop the grassy knoll at the time of the assassination. Sylvia Meagher states flatly that he was "one of the assassins,"[15] while Robert Groden takes another tact. He calls the entire Secret Service a "suspect" in the assassination itself.[16] I've heard other explanations ranging from zombie CIA agents to time travelers. None makes much sense.

As we'll see later in this book, if the "Secret Service agent" were an assassin, he was either poorly trained or poorly equipped for the task. He would have failed to hit the Presidential limousine or any of its occupants from a distance of just more than one hundred feet.

Returning for the moment to Mrs. Hill's account, the "puff of smoke" she says she observed was, in fact, seen by other witnesses as well. Sam Holland, Frank Reilly, Austin Miller, James Simmons and Clemmon Johnson were all standing on the triple overpass as the motorcade approached. Holland turns up as one of Mark Lane's star witnesses in *Rush to Judgment*.*

I have no doubt that these men saw smoke rising from the trees near the corner of the wooden fence. I have, on several different occasions, noticed identical smoke there myself. It is generated by automobile exhaust when a car parked near the fence is started or idled. Doubtless, once this book is in print, some critics will criticize this conclusion and conjecture that the auto in question was in some way connected with the assassination. I can't prove that it wasn't, nor can the critics prove that the smoke came from a weapon. In view of the medical evidence, I believe mine to be the more logical explanation. But, as we've seen, many critics aren't interested in logic—just lurid speculation.

Smoke from the trees atop the knoll . . . fleeing gunmen that witnesses will dodge speeding cars to pursue . . . the question comes to mind: Was there someone in back of the knoll who observed that area at the time of the assassination? Indeed there was. He was Lee Bowers, Jr., stationed behind the grassy knoll in the second story of a railroad signal tower. Bowers' location was due west of the Depository.

Remember the flash of light Jean Hill has appended to her eyewitness testimony? Well, Bowers saw it too—or, at least, Mark Lane got him to say so. Bowers saw two men standing near the fence just before the shots were fired. He said one was middle-aged and fairly heavy-set. The other was about mid-twenties in either a plaid shirt or plaid coat or jacket.[18]

---

* Later, Holland called Lane "too far out for me." [17]

In *Rush to Judgment* Bowers continued to tell about the area behind the fence:

> *"At the time of the shooting, in the vicinity of where the two men I have described were, there was a flash of light, or, as far as I am concerned, something I could not identify, but . . . which caught my eye in this immediate area of the embankment. Now what this was, I . . . could not identify it, other than some unusual occurrence–a flash of light or smoke or something which caused me to feel like something out of the ordinary had occurred there."*[19]

It's worth noting that Bowers didn't mention any sort of "out of the ordinary" occurrence in his deposition filed just after the assassination.[20] He did recall seeing "some commotion" there when he testified before the Warren Commission in April, 1964.[21]

Then, Bowers told the Commission that he was "unable to describe" what he saw,[22] rather than it was something out of the ordinary, a "sort of milling around, but something occurred in this particular spot which was out of the ordinary, which attracted my eye for some reason, which I could not identify."[23] In *Rush to Judgment*, Lane leaves out the phrase "a sort of milling around" which was the closest Bowers could come to describing what had caught his attention. Assistant Commission Counsel Joe Ball asked Bowers twice to describe the "commotion" and twice before the end of his testimony if he remembered anything more about the incident. Ball was unable to elicit further information.

What exactly did Bowers see? The Warren Commission published a photograph depicting his view from the signal tower behind the wooden fence, but the Commissioners and staff never actually climbed into the tower. If they had, they would have noticed something most unusual—something that would cast substantial doubt on the strength of Bower's testimony. Bowers testified that he was extremely busy at the time of the assassination.[24] His work position required him to throw signal switches located on a panel in the center of the room. Sitting at the panel, Bowers could not have seen the area at the apex of the wooden fence where Lane and Meagher, among others, place their mythical assassin. Bowers, in order to view the area in question from a window somewhat removed from his control panel, would have had to leave his switches and walk over to the window. By all accounts, Bowers was a good employee, not a shirker of duty. It is inconceivable to me that he walked away from his control panel at a particularly busy time to stare at the back of a picket fence.* Indeed, Bowers testified that he "threw red-on-red"—a signal that effectively blocked all trains—just after the fatal shot. He had to be sitting at his control panel to take this action.[25]

As far as I'm able to determine, no other critic or researcher was interested enough in the signal tower until Sixth Floor project consultant Carl Henry went into the building with a video recorder in the summer of 1988. Henry (who, unlike me, believes that there's "something being hidden"[26] about the assassination) told me simply, "There's no way Bowers could have seen what he said he saw."[27]

Counsel Ball then asked Bowers if he had familiarity with sounds coming from both locations. Bowers replied that he "had worked this same tower for ten or twelve years and was there during the time they were renovating the School Depository Building and had noticed at that time the similarity of sounds occurring in either of these two locations. There is a similarity of sound because there is a reverberation which takes place from either location." [28]

Predictably, Mark Lane, Sylvia Meagher, Josiah Thompson, and virtually every other published critic has ignored this portion of Bowers' testimony. Yet it is more valuable than the recounting of the "commotion" he witnessed behind the fence.

In the next chapter, we'll see that the weight of hard, physical evidence indicates that three shots were fired from the Texas School Book Depository building. But what about witnesses who heard shots from the grassy knoll?

Again, the Plaza is a vast echo chamber. I made the same statement at the beginning of this chapter without giving it much weight. Various individuals in various locations heard various sounds. Some thought the shots were backfires. Others thought they came from high above. Still others looked toward the knoll. In *Six Seconds in Dallas*, Josiah Thompson arranged an overall profile of witness testimony. Of sixty-four witnesses who gave an opinion as to where the shots originated, thirty-three pointed to the grassy knoll. Another twenty-five pin-

---

* Bowers, incidentally, was asked by Counsel Ball about the source of the three shots he heard. Bowers replied that the sounds "came either from up against the School Depository Building or near the mouth of the triple underpass." Bowers could not say which was the actual source. [29]

pointed the Depository. Two claimed the gunfire erupted from the east side of Houston Street from among the County buildings. And four witnesses heard noises from two directions.[30]

Taking Dr. Thompson at his word,* we can look further in his book to his chart depicting the positions of nearly two hundred witnesses in Dealey Plaza at the time of the assassination. We can only assume that the more than sixty witnesses Thompson used in his profile are represented here, because several score are not.[31] Additionally, the chart itself contains important and glaring errors. In consulting with the Sixth Floor exhibit coordinators, I mentioned that Thompson must not have seen the chart artwork until after it had been printed. Why he didn't correct it for the paperback edition of his book is beyond me.[32]

At any rate, the geographic distribution of eyewitnesses is about even east-to-west. A number are clustered near the front of the Depository, several are on the overpass, and still others line the streets of the Plaza. Generally speaking, where an eyewitness stood affected what he or she thought they heard.

I told my clients in my sales training business that "what you and I feel, think, or hear has no relation to the real world," meaning that others will interpret those things differently. It is a sentiment that applies to the assassination as well.

Interestingly enough, witnesses who became central figures in critics' books didn't support shots fired from the knoll. Sam Holland, on the triple overpass, (the eyewitness who saw the puff of smoke and became Mark Lane's bright and shining star) said he thought the first two or three shots of the four he heard came from further up Elm Street. Counsel for the Warren Commission asked Holland if he thought that the shots were coming from near the underpass. Holland's one-word reply, "No."[34]

I don't have to tell you that this particular quote is neither in Mark Lane's book nor in Thompson's. In *Six Seconds in Dallas*, Thompson devotes four pages to Holland, much of it detailing the hokum that an assassin might have fired the fatal shot, then hidden himself in a car

---

* *We have to take Dr. Thompson, a professor turned private investigator, at his word. Although he was always ready to aid our efforts on the Sixth Floor project, he will not talk to me. The last time I called him, he hung up.[33]*

trunk and slammed the lid shut before witnesses arrived behind the knoll.[35]

Abraham Zapruder, the Dallas dress manufacturer who took the famous motion picture of the assassination, told investigators that the shots came from behind him. The corner of the wooden fence was to Zapruder's right front. Half the world was behind him, including the Texas School Book Depository.*

Witnesses in the motorcade moving down Elm Street between the Depository and the grassy knoll agreed almost to a man that the shots were fired from the building, and not from the incline in front of them. Thirteen out of fifteen witnesses questioned said that the shots came from above, not street level. Yet in *Rush to Judgment*, Mark Lane suggests that we ignore this mass of testimony "because of the obvious possibility that it might be colored." [36]

Colored? Just because the witnesses happened to be government employees or their spouses? Who might have colored their testimony, and for what purpose? Mr. Lane doesn't provide the answer, just the question.

I daresay that witnesses riding in the motorcade were among the very best witnesses upon which to base a theory of the origin of the gunfire. They were moving from in front of one potential source to the other, immune from the shouts and cries of the spectators in the Plaza, and accustomed enough to being around the President of the United States that they did not focus all their attention on Mr. Kennedy.

Yet, Mark Lane says this is precisely the kind of testimony you should ignore.

Perhaps Lane should also discount the rooftop interview he conducted with Jesse Price, since Price told investigators that he heard a final shot five minutes after the first volley of gunfire. Of course, you won't find the statement in Lane's book.[37]

A few other notes about the grassy knoll and its fictive assassin are in order before we proceed to a discussion of the physical evidence in this case. One thing Lane and the other critics never bother to mention

---

* *Robert Anson in* They Killed the President *details Zapruder's experience to include feeling a "bullet whistle past his right ear." [38] Anson invented the entire phrase. No such comment exists among Zapruder's testimony, deposition, or published statements.*

in their books is that the parking lot behind the grassy knoll was used, in late 1963, for Sheriff's Office employees. One could hardly pick a more inopportune location for a Presidential assassin.[39] Another thing you rarely find are photos taken from behind the fence itself. There's good reason for this omission. The critics don't want you to know that the grassy knoll afforded a would-be assassin only a cross-shot—meaning that the target moved across his field of vision from left to right rather than directly away, which is the more preferable of the two. Firing from atop the knoll would hardly have been the choice of the discriminating assassin.

The next thing you'll never read in critical literature is the fact that no shell casings were found behind the fence.* While there were footprints in that location, there was nothing at all to indicate the presence of an assassin.

Of course, the critics maintain that this circumstance is just as it should be. They cite their widespread belief that no assassin would deliberately leave a tell-tale sign like a shell casing lying about. Well, assuming a grassy knoll assassin did have the presence of mind to pick up an empty shell casing, why didn't anyone see the gunman himself? Why didn't anyone see his rifle? Why did he pick such a poor vantage point from which to fire at the President? Why would he fire and run with witnesses standing on a stairway only yards away?[40] Most damning of all, why didn't this putative assassin manage to hit the President, any of the other occupants, or some part of the massive Presidential limousine from a range of 110 feet?[41] And assuming that he was a poor enough shot to miss everyone and everything, where did the bullet go?

Quite plainly, the critics have had a field day atop the grassy knoll. They've searched for decades for a gunman who never was. Pulitzer Prize-winning author John Toland has said "Everyone's looking for the smoking gun. And nobody's found it. But just because they can't find the smoking gun doesn't mean one wasn't there."[43] Indeed.

Robert Groden, in High Treason, *captions a photo of the knoll scene with the statement that there are unconfirmed reports of an empty bullet shell.* [42] *Groden fails to provide the source of any evidence to support these "unconfirmed reports." I've been researching this case for twenty-three years, and I've never heard of them.*

1. Sylvia Meagher, *Accessories After the Fact*, (Bobbs-Merrill, 1967), 15.
2. Ibid.
3. Lane, 25
4. Ibid.
5. Ibid.
6. United Press International, *Four Days*, (American Heritage, 1964), 20-21.
7. *USA Today* television program, February 20, 1989.
8. Letter to the author, June 19, 1977.
9. 6H, 210-215.
10. Anthony Summers, *Conspiracy*, (McGraw Hill, 1980), 81.
11. Josiah Thompson, *Six Seconds in Dallas*, (Berkley, 1976), 129.
12. Business card given to the author, November 22, 1988.
13. Summers, Ibid.
14. Meagher, 25.
15. Ibid., 26
16 Robert Groden and Harrison Livingston, *High Treason*, (Conservatory Press, 1989), 137.
17. Charles Roberts, *The Truth About the Assassination*, (Grosset & Dunlap, 1967), 122.
18. Lane, 23.
19. Ibid., 24.
20. Roberts, 32.
21. Ibid.
22. Ibid.
23. Ibid., 33.
24. 6H, 288; Roberts, 30.
25. Jim Bishop, *The Day Kennedy Was Shot*, (Funk & Wagnalls, 1968), 158.
26. *USA Today*, Ibid.
27. Conversation with the author, July 27, 1988.
28. 6H, 288.
29. Ibid.
30. David Lifton, *Best Evidence*, (Macmillian, 1980), 37.
31. Ibid., 316.
32. Most glaring is the misplacement of one of Thompson's key photographic witnesses—Phil Willis. He was standing southwest of Hugh Betzner (also shown on the chart) and is clearly visible in Zapruder film frames just before the limousine disappears behind the roadway sign. Betzner is standing a good twenty feet to Willis' right, and somewhat behind him–not in front.
33. Attempted conversation with Dr. Thompson, September 26, 1978.
34. Roberts, 33.
35. Thompson, 160.
36. Lane, 29.
37. 19H, 492.
38. Robert Anson, *They've Killed the President!*, (Bantam, 1976), 26.
39. Roberts, 32.
40. Dealey Plaza groundskeeper Emmett Hudson was one of the closest witnesses to the wooden fence. He was about fifteen feet from the fence corner, and standing on the stairway which ranges down the side of the grassy knoll. Excellent photos of Hudson in this portion are found in the Nix and Muchmore film frames published in UPI's *Four Days*.
41. Measured in Dealey Plaza, from corner of the fence to approximate position of President Kennedy at the moment of the fatal head shot.
42. Groden and Livingston, Ibid., first photo section.
43. Toland made this comment regarding the Japanese sneak attack on Pearl Harbor, and not regarding the assassination.

IV

At the Depository— The Physical Evidence

No one knows why Dallas police officers took a half-hour to find the sniper's nest on the southeast corner of the sixth floor. Indeed, the Texas School Book Depository remained unsealed for several minutes following the assassination, allowing Oswald to saunter back up Elm Street and board a waiting bus. Although several witnesses had told officers that they had seen a gunman in the sixth floor window, the area wasn't identified as a possible crime site until 1 p.m.[1]

Deputy Luke Mooney squeezed through Oswald's "shield" of book boxes and immediately saw three things of interest: first, a trio of book cartons stacked so as to serve as a rifle rest on and near the window ledge; second, three spent shells, and third, a brown paper bag—not the kind you'd find at a grocery store, but rather one which appeared longish and handmade.[2]

Minutes after Mooney secured the southeast corner window, another deputy discovered a bolt-action rifle hidden between and underneath stacks of book boxes at the opposite corner of the sixth floor. After determining that the quality of wood in the rifle stock was too poor to retain fingerprints, detective J.C. Day lifted the rifle from its hiding place and held it while Police Captain Will Fritz worked the bolt and ejected a live round from the rifle chamber.[3]

Lt. Day allowed no other officers to handle the rifle, but instead retained possession of the firearm and took it to Dallas Police headquarters for processing as evidence.[4]

Throughout the afternoon of the assassination, newspaper reporters and law enforcement officials crowded into the sniper's nest at the southeast corner window, taking photo after photo and altering the arrangement of book boxes that had shielded the assassin from view.

There is no evidence that officers conducted any further search of the floor after the discovery of the gunman's lair and the rifle itself. Indeed, Oswald's clipboard was not found until early December although it was sitting less than ten feet from the location of the rifle.[5] Incidentally, none of the orders on the clipboard had been filled. In justifying their theories and criticisms, assassination researchers have variously interpreted each piece of sixth floor evidence: the rifle, the shells, the boxes, the paper bag, and the clipboard.

Sylvia Meagher suggests that officers conducted a thorough search of the floor, and that the clipboard was planted prior to its discovery on December 2 in an effort to incriminate Oswald.[6] And while the sixth floor was swarming with reporters and law enforcement officers, the high and haphazard stacks of book cartons made a conventional search almost impossible. Indeed, Ms. Meagher suggests that the sixth floor was an unlikely place for the assassin to have secreted himself. She suggests that a sixth-floor sniper's perch rings false in view of the equal accessibility and nearly deserted state of the seventh floor of the Depository.

In *Accessories After the Fact*, Ms. Meagher wrote: "Far less risk would attach to the seventh floor—not only was it deserted, but, according to the diagram, there is an enclosure at the southeast corner that would ensure privacy at the southeast corner window."[7]

It is obvious Ms. Meagher never took the time or trouble to visit the seventh floor and view the area for herself. There was indeed an enclosure around the southeast corner window, and the area had once been used as a separate office. I fought unsuccessfully to keep the Dallas County work crews from dismantling it when they poured concrete over the weak wooden floor.

The enclosure was only fiberboard nailed to studs. This would have been sufficient for concealment were it not for the door through which one gained access to the small office. The door was fitted with a large window, although the glass was probably knocked out long before the assassination.* When I first visited the seventh floor, the

---

* *I have spent a good deal of time on the seventh floor in an effort to convince the County to allow me to use the space as a work area in which to reassemble the Hertz rent-a-car sign that formerly stood on the Depository roof.*

fiberboard walls had been severely damaged and partially torn away as well. Whether this condition existed at the time of the assassination is a matter of conjecture. In any case, the door was certainly in place, so an assassin using the southeast corner window of the seventh floor would have been liable to discovery by anyone who happened up the corner stairway.

Additionally, the window sills on the seventh floor were built considerably higher than those on the sixth, which extend only a few bricks above floor level. On floor seven, the sills come up to my waist, and would prove uncomfortable when used as a rifle rest. I've experimented using a long stick!

A ledge runs along the top of the sixth floor, and extends some distance into the field of sight for a seventh-floor assassin. The gunman would have been forced to lean some distance into the window sill in order to sight on the limousine below. Thus, he would have been readily observable by witnesses at ground level.

The sixth floor, on the other hand, offered no such difficulties. Of all the vantage points in the Depository, the southeast corner window appears best today, just as it did on the day of the assassination. Ms. Meagher's theory shows that, like most critics, she wouldn't know a good vantage point from a poor one. Even a cursory examination of the Depository does great damage to her theory. Ms. Meagher went on to add that the assassin probably experienced difficulty in moving the cartons of books to form the small fortress which hid him from view. In her words: ". . . the alleged assassin assembled a shield consisting of some twenty four cartons, each of which weighed about fifty pounds, most of which had to be lifted physically and placed atop one, two, or three other cartons. This would require substantial exertion and considerable time."[8]

Actually the assassin lifted and placed far more than two dozen book cartons. The re-creation Rick Lane and I completed required more than a hundred boxes. Not all of these need have been moved by the assassin, however.

Ms. Meagher mentions that floor–laying crews were busy on the sixth floor during the week of the assassination,[9] but she gives the point no weight. In reality, the crews had not laid a plywood covering over the southeast corner area, and had instead moved boxes of books from other, more central floor areas out into the fringes of the sixth floor storage space. Thus, many of the boxes the assassin stacked for his shield might well have been in place or nearly placed, and thus required little or no effort on the part of the gunman. I believe that the assassin built the shield sometime during the early morning hours on the day of the assassination. Likely, the shield served as a place of concealment for his rifle until the gunman occupied it during the noon hour.

The boxes themselves, weighing little more than fifty pounds each, would have been easily moved by someone of average strength.

The shield itself had three basic components: First, a stack of cartons running parallel to the east window of the southeast corner, presumably, to guard against spectators in the Dal-Tex building across the street looking into the corner and seeing the assassin; second, a multi-stack arrangement that effectively screened the area from others working on the sixth floor, and third, the shield itself which served as a backdrop for the assassin and faced the southern wall of the building. These, then, were the boxes photographed by press photographers and spectators just before and immediately after the shots were fired. As is evident from our reconstruction, the assassin had carefully arranged the cartons to cover all angles by which he might be detected.

I believe that, after firing the shots, the gunman walked out of the shield by turning to his right and continuing along the eastern wall of the Depository for a few yards, then turning left and heading diagonally across the floor. I am about the same height and weight as Lee Harvey Oswald, and I had no difficulty in exiting the sniper's nest in this manner.

Ms. Meagher, however, claims that entering and exiting the shield of cartons would have required additional time and would have meant that the assassin would have disturbed the arrangement of cartons on his way out of the area. [10]

Ms. Meagher's assertion is incorrect. Rick and I placed those cartons within a half-inch of their original position. Marks on the old wooden floor, covered by plywood a few days after the assassination, were again visible when we removed the plywood to prepare the exhibit.

Those same marks appeared in several of the photos we used as aids in re-creating the scene. Since there was no way for those marks to move during the twenty-five years they were covered over, they served as extremely accurate guides for placement of the boxes.*

The wrapping-paper bag found near the window must have been fashioned by the assassin the afternoon prior to the assassination and used to carry the murder weapon into the Depository on the morning of the crime. There are, however, problems with any hypothesis regarding the paper bag. First, it was not photographed in place as it was discovered. Second, although the outside of the bag contained Oswald's palm print, there were no oil stains on the bag and precious little in the way of fibers or traces to connect the rifle with the bag. Third, both of the witnesses who saw Oswald with a long and bulky package on the morning of the assassination recall the package as being about twenty-seven inches long. The disassembled rifle would have been at least thirty-five inches long, the length of the wooden stock. [11]

Critic Robert Groden has suggested another explanation for the brown paper bag: "It would seem, therefore, that the cops found a bag in the junk-pile on the sixth floor and turned it over as evidence to the FBI since there was no other way of explaining how Oswald had brought in the gun . . . "[12]

What Mr. Groden neglected to do was to check to see if there was a junk-pile on the sixth floor. In a brief conversation with Depository Superintendent Roy Truly during the summer of 1974, I asked him if there was any sort of collection of garbage, waste, or castoffs on floor six. His two-word reply: "Absolutely not." [13] In a word, Mr. Truly ran a clean ship.

The only explanation for the paper bag (unless you accept a carefully spun web to entrap young Oswald) is that it was used to carry the Mannlicher-Carcano into the Depository. I believe that Oswald manufactured the bag (the paper was proven to have come from the Depository shipping department) at the Depository prior to leaving for the Paine residence in Irving on the afternoon before the assassination. And I believe, as the Warren Commission did, that Wes Frazier and his

---

Markings on the floor are even more evident in the corner stairway area, where I was able to place the position of the rifle with great precision.

sister (Wes was the young man who gave Oswald a ride to and from Irving) were genuinely mistaken about the length of the bag.

Since Oswald's palm print was found on the bottom of the bag, it not only meant that he had handled the bag, but that it had been used to carry something bulky or heavy. In view of the fact that Oswald told Frazier the bag contained curtain rods Oswald should have been able to carry the container with his fingertips.[14]

No curtain rods were ever found in the Depository. They probably would have been easy enough to locate. Based on the way Oswald carried the paper bag, it would have had to contain some pretty stout curtain rods.

As I pointed out in Chapter One, the easiest answer to critics who complain of inconsistencies in the paper bag theory is to ask them a question for a change. Do they really think Oswald carried curtain rods to work that day? And if so, why? Contrary to another of Robert Groden's unsubstantiated statements, Oswald's rented room in the Oak Cliff section of Dallas didn't need curtain rods, nor was he allowed to make changes in its decor.[15]

The three cartridge cases found along the south window in the southeast corner have drawn much attention. All had been fired in Oswald's rifle. In *Six Seconds in Dallas*, Josiah Thompson makes much of the fact that one of the cartridge cases had a dented lip, making it impossible for the casing to hold a bullet.[16] Thompson's dark surmise: Oswald's rifle could only have fired two shots that day, and not three as the Warren Commission determined.

The dent on the cartridge case, however, is typical of a mark made when the empty brass casing is re-inserted into the rifle breech. I have dented several casings in this manner when I inserted them, empty, into my own Carcano. Thompson cites the dented cartridge lip as more "irrefutable evidence that Oswald could not have killed JFK alone." [17] The dented lip proves no such thing. It only suggests that a curious police investigator wanted to make sure the cartridge fit in Oswald's rifle. Yet Thompson, in an apparent effort to impress readers with sheer volume of research, devotes five pages to the question of the dented cartridge case.[18]

The discovery of the assassin's rifle in the Depository has been the subject of much writing. In *Rush to Judgment* Mark Lane devotes an entire chapter to the question of what type of rifle was actually found.[19] As Josiah Thompson put it, "Lane leaves the implication with his readers that the Dallas authorities fiddled the evidence . . . "[20]

The rifle found on the sixth floor was a military-surplus, bolt-action, clip-fed carbine fitted with a four-power telescopic sight. Photos and motion pictures exist of the rifle's discovery and its subsequent removal from the building. The confusion arises because of how the weapon was identified.

The rifle was found by Deputy Constable Seymour Weitzman, along with Deputy Sheriff Eugene Boone. The two men were shortly joined by Deputy Sheriff Luke Mooney, who had discovered the southeast corner window firing site.[21] The discovery of the weapon occurred at 1:22 p.m.[22]

In a statement he made to the Dallas Police Department on the day after the assassination, Deputy Weitzman called the rifle a "7.65 Mauser bolt action with a 4/8 scope, (with) a thick leather brownish sling on it."[23] The Mannlicher-Carcano subsequently removed from the Depository has "Made Italy" and "Cal 6.5" stamped on the rounded top of the receiver, along with the weapon's serial number, C-2766.[24]

Assistant Warren Commission Counsel Joseph Ball tried to put the matter to rest on April 1, 1964, when he took Weitzman's sworn deposition:

> Ball: *"In a statement that you made to the Dallas Police Department that afternoon, you referred to the rifle as a 7.65 Mauser bolt action?"*
>
> Weitzman: *"In a glance that's what it looked like."*[25]

Josiah Thompson notes: "The Mauser and the Carcano do resemble each other. Weitzman's error would seem to be just what he called it, "an honest mistake." [26] But critics and sensationalists have been reluctant to let the matter die there. The result is considerable public confusion over what kind of rifle was actually found in the Depository. Indeed, there should be no confusion at all, especially since motion pictures and still photographs clearly show that the rifle being discovered and removed is a Mannlicher-Carcano.[27] *

---

*Sylvia Meagher wrote that the identity of the rifle "still awaits a conclusive determination," apparently without mentioning relevant photos and footage. [28]

At the height of the assassination controversy in the mid-1970s, Robert Groden wrote:

> *". . . We learn that when the assassin's rifle was first discovered in the Book Depository, the two officers who found it testified it was a 7.65 mm German-made Mauser, only to abruptly change their story a day later, raising the possibility that there may have been, in fact, two rifles found. Or that a switch had been made for some insidious purpose."* [29]

Apparently, when one adopts Groden's train of thought, one can truthfully say that ". . . there is just too much in this case that defies logic . . ." [30]

The rifle itself is fairly straightforward. The Mannlicher-Carcano was made in Italy, at Terni, in 1940. It was imported into the United States as Italian Military surplus, and was sold at an extremely inexpensive quantity price. Oswald sent away for the weapon with which he would kill the President. He purchased the rifle for $21.45 [31] and had C-2766 shipped to "A. Hidell" at Post Office Box 2915 in Dallas on March 20, 1963. The envelope, order form, and money order used to purchase the rifle were filled out and addressed by Lee Harvey Oswald. [32]

Found still in the rifle mechanism was a six-shot clip or bullet holder. The last round of ammunition had been pushed up out of the clip and into the firing chamber. Apparently, the assassin had worked the bolt action by reflex after he fired the shot which struck President Kennedy in the back of the head.

Sylvia Meagher notes that the Carcano usually ejects its clip when all ammunition has been fired and the last round has been driven into the chamber. [33] Had Ms. Meagher journeyed to the National Archives to test Oswald's rifle, she would have discovered that this particular weapon retains the clip. [34] Indeed, photos of detective Day carrying the rifle out of the Depository show the clip clearly in place inside the trigger housing. [35]

Much has been written about the Mannlicher-Carcano carbine; maligning the weapon has been a favorite sport of the critics. They view it as an odd choice for a Presidential assassin. And it was. A more sophisticated gunman would not have settled for a 23-year-old Italian Army surplus rifle.

In *Kennedy and Lincoln*, Dr. John K. Lattimer wrote:

"That Oswald used weapons of such low cost, and therefore of marginal dependability, was impressive additional evidence to me that he was not in the pay of anyone else. He clearly financed his own weapons out of his own pocket with his own meager funds. He was independent in this, as in everything else he did."[36]

But the critics don't tell you that anyone desiring to find a patsy for the assassination of the President would surely have sought someone who owned a better rifle. They merely contend that Oswald could not have used the weapon to do what the Warren Commission said he did. Ballistics evidence aside (we'll discuss the bullet wounds in later chapters), Oswald looked down on a slowly moving target and fired at that target as it went away from him. The shot was not difficult. Indeed, the more I stood in the sixth-floor window, the easier Oswald's feat became. That same conclusion is not likely to be reached either from the next set of windows or from street level.

William Manchester wrote in *Death of a President* that Oswald had managed to find the perfect location from which to fire: "At that range, and with his skill, he could scarcely have missed." [37]

I believe that Oswald took nearly seven seconds to fire three shots. The Carcano rifle bolt can be operated in 2.3 seconds between shots, without allowing much time to sight in on the target. Hence, my conviction that, even with the Mannlicher-Carcano, Oswald could have fired fast enough to do what the Commission claimed he did.[38] Practice with the weapon's bolt action was an all-important key, and Oswald apparently availed himself of many opportunities to work the bolt and to sight imaginary targets while familiarizing himself with the Carcano in his screened-in back porch.[39]

Critics have complained that the telescopic sight mounted on the Carcano was misaligned, and thus, defective.[40] The Warren Commission, on the other hand, alleged that the scope defect would have aided the assassin as his target moved away from him.[41] As FBI firearms expert Robert Frazier told Counsel:

"The fact that the cross hairs are set high would actually compensate for any lead which had to be taken. So that if you aimed with this weapon as it actually was received at the laboratory, it would not be necessary to take any lead whatsoever in order to hit the intended object. The scope would

accomplish the lead for you."[42]

My own Carcano, manufactured in the same arsenal as was Oswald's and only a thousand rifles before his, is anything but a "cheap old weapon," as FBI fingerprint expert Sebastian Latona described it before the Warren Commission.[43] Critics have seized upon this comment and have quite literally milked it for millions. I suspect that Latona, who was concerned with the latent palm print discovered on the rifle barrel, was referring to the quality of the wood stock as "cheap" and "old," and it is. Admittedly Oswald's rifle in the National Archives is somewhat worse for wear than mine.

As a firearm, though, the Carcano is a formidable and accurate weapon. The bolt-action on the C-2766 demanded a strong and muscular forearm to operate it efficiently and quickly; Oswald possessed such strength in his upper arms.[44] The flawed telescopic sight, tragically enough, actually aided him in the assassination. He had practiced enough with the rifle to become thoroughly familiar with it, something the experts who later test fired it at targets weren't permitted to do.[45]

And here's something no critic ever mentions: the rifle Oswald used to kill the President had a muzzle velocity of over two thousand feet per second.[46] We don't use carbines with that kind of strength in the United States Army.[47]

You'll see in later chapters that this extremely high muzzle velocity answers numerous questions about bullet wounds—questions critics have raised and left unanswered over the past quarter of a century.

Predictably, most critics who disparage the Mannlicher-Carcano have never held such a rifle in their hands. Josiah Thompson refrains from criticism of the weapon; it is obvious that he has spent considerable time handling a rifle similar to Oswald's. On the other hand, Robert Groden, whom I regard as one of the most irresponsible critics ever to put paper in a typewriter, labeled the weapon as "eccentric."[48]

The Carcano, then, while not the choice of a discriminating presidential assassin, is reliable, accurate, and solid. To say less of it would be to do the weapon a disservice. The rifle was equipped with an unusual leather sling, which Oswald most probably cannibalized from an old-style Air Force issue holster belt.[49]

Sylvia Meagher raised a disconcerting spectre in *Accessories After the Fact*, namely, that Oswald's rifle might not be the only one of its type bearing the serial number, C-2766. The clear implication was that the real assassins had searched the four corners of the earth to find another Carcano with the same serial number as the one ordered by Oswald, then planted it in the Depository to incriminate Oswald as the assassin. What the conspirators managed to do with Oswald's rifle remained a small mystery.

It is correct that the Italian government may have created a number of Carcanos bearing the serial number "2766."[50] But C-2766 was the only weapon bearing a "C" in the serial number. An FBI report on the subject reads: "Since many concerns were manufacturing the same weapon, the same serial number appears on weapons manufactured by more than one concern. Some bear a letter prefix and some do not."[51]

The problem with Ms. Meagher's allegation lies in the fact that the name of the production plant manufacturing C-2766 is stamped on the top of the receiver. I have yet to find a Carcano without a stamped plant of manufacture. The letter "C" as a prefix would have been used at Terni where Oswald's carbine was made and at no other plant. The closest another serial number might have come would have been "UC2766" made at the Beretta concern in Gardone.[52]

Again, particularly in Ms. Meagher's case, it was easier for her to foster the charge than to do the research.

Any discussion of the physical evidence found at the Depository would be incomplete without reference to one of the most absurd allegations of all—that Oswald did not have sufficient time in which to exit his shield of book cartons, run across the sixth floor and secret his rifle, dash down eight small flights of stairs, and enter the Depository lunchroom in time to be seen and stopped there by Dallas Police Officer, Marrion L. Baker and Superintendent Truly, all within two minutes of the fatal shot.*

The problem with the reconstruction of Oswald's movements is two-fold: First, no shield of cartons existed around the southeast corner window when the Warren Commission conducted its re-enactment, and no cartons had been arranged as a hiding place for the rifle near the

---

* *Sylvia Meagher, the standard of accuracy on which most critics rely, refers to Officer Baker as "M.S."*[53]

corner stairway. The weapon was simply dropped on the floor.

Secondly, now that the carton shield and corner stairway area have both been re-created, there's a bigger problem: one would have to zig-zag around exhibit panels on a trek across the floor, and the corner stairway itself no longer exists.*

When the County purchased the old Book Depository in the late 1970s, workmen constructed a new stairway made of steel in the northeast corner of the building, or down the east wall from the corner window. Then, in 1987, workmen removed the last vestiges of the original northwest corner staircase. What visitors see today is a carefully preserved illusion—the staircase that appears to descend from six to five goes only halfway down, and the exit from the staircase onto the seventh floor has been sealed off forever.

Despite these difficulties or, rather, because of them, Secret Service agent John Howlett was able to duplicate the route of the assassin in seventy-three and seventy-four seconds on his first and second attempts, respectively.[54]

Officer Baker's two tries, reconstructing stopping his motorcycle, running to the front of the building, and making his way with Mr. Truly to the second floor—required ninety seconds and seventy-five seconds, respectively.[55] To his credit, Officer Baker was careful to point out that, on the day of the assassination, "it took me a little longer."[56]

I am not a fast runner. At any rate, making allowances for the missing stairwell, and starting and stopping the timing accordingly, I was able to exit the shield of cartons, hide the rifle where Oswald hid it, and run down the new staircase to the second floor, then walk to the approximate location of the old lunchroom . . . all within ninety-one seconds.

Oswald had just entered the lunchroom doors when Baker caught sight of him. Thus, to my satisfaction (based on Baker's own reconstruction in 1964) he could have gotten there fast enough. What the critics don't tell you is that, in descending the staircase four floors to the lunchroom, Oswald walked down a grand total of seventy-two steps. Walking across the sixth floor and hiding the rifle took longer than

---

* *The pieces of the stairway, however, are in storage.*

walking down the stairs.[57]

After the encounter with Baker and Truly in the lunchroom, Oswald (displaying icy calm even though Baker was holding a revolver at Oswald's midsection) put a nickel in the soda machine and selected a Coca-Cola. It may be that this single action on Oswald's part holds the key to his guilt. Oswald habitually drank Dr Pepper.[58] There can be only one realistic explanation for a miser like Oswald to fail to select his soft drink of choice—he was nervous. Three other possibilities exist, all unlikely:

1. *Oswald really bought a Dr Pepper and every witness questioned recalled it as a Coca-Cola.*
2. *The soda machine was out of Dr Pepper.*
3. *The soda machine—a Coca-Cola Company product—malfunctioned in favor of its manufacturer.*

Mr. Truly ensured Oswald's escape from the Depository by identifying him to Officer Baker as an employee. Oswald purchased his Coca-Cola and no doubt mentally kicked himself for wasting a nickel, then made his way out of the building. Sylvia Meagher chides him for taking his own sweet time:

"At that moment Oswald had merely to return to the back stairs, walk down one flight to the first floor, and walk out the back door. The longer he delayed, the greater the danger that the building would be sealed off by the police . . ."[59]

Apparently Ms. Meagher believes Oswald would have broken and run if he had just committed the assassination. After mis-purchasing his Coca-Cola, Oswald walked across the second floor, down the front stairway, and out the main entrance. On his way out, he directed radio reporter Pierce Allman to a telephone.[60] The icy calm Oswald displayed would serve him well again, in less than forty-five minutes.

1. Meagher, 41.
2. WCR, 127.
3. WCR, 85.
4. UPI, Ibid., 29, and Thompson, Ibid., 279.
5. Distance measured during reconstruction of corner staircase area, February 1989.
6. Meagher, 69.
7. Ibid., 43.
8. Ibid., 44.
9. Ibid., 43.
10. Ibid., 44.
11. Measurement of the authors Carcano, Serial No. C 1551.
12. Groden and Peter Model, *JFK—The Case for Conspiracy*, (Manor Books, 1976), 265.
13. Telephone interview with Roy Truly, conducted by the author.
14. WCR, 130. The bag also contained Oswald's left index fingerprint.
15. David Belin, *November 22, 1963: You Are the Jury*, (Quadrangle Books, 1973), 468.
16. Thompson, 192.
17. Ibid., cover of paperback edition.
18. Ibid., 191-195.
19. Lane, 95.
20. Thompson, 277.
21. Meagher, 41.
22. WCR, 85.
23. Thompson, 277.
24. WCR, 85-86.
25. 7H, 103.
26. Thompson, 279.
27. Dallas' KERA television program, *Special Edition*, commemorated the opening of the Sixth Floor Exhibit during its February 17, 1989 telecast. The program featured Rick Lane and me as we began reconstruction of the southeast corner window. Also featured was vintage news footage from WFAA-TV, depicting Police Detective J.C. Day carefully brushing the just-found rifle for fingerprints. Even in black-and-white, the weapon is obviously a Carcano. The gun's clip is visible lying on a book box just behind the rifle.
28. Meagher, 100.
29. Groden and Model, 29.
30. Ibid.
31. WCR, 114.
32. Ibid.
33. Meagher, 113.
34. Dr. John K. Lattimer, *Kennedy and Lincoln*, (Harcourt-Brace-Jovanovich, 1980), 299.
35. UPI, *Four Days*, (American Heritage, 1964), 29.
36. Lattimer, 334.
37. Manchester, 95.
38. Lattimer, 304.
39. Ibid., 139.
40. Meagher, 107.
41. WCR, 182.
42. Ibid.
43. Meagher, 101.
44. Lattimer, 304.
45. WCR, 181.
46. Ibid.
47. Jim Bishop on ABC TV, *Good Night America*, May 29, 1975.
48. Groden and Model, 27.
49. Lattimer, 297.
50. Meagher, 105.

51. Ibid.
52. Based on the author's Carcano, manufactured in 1940 at Gardone, Italy.
53. Meagher, 43.
54. WCR, 142.
55. Ibid.
56. Ibid., 143.
57. Bishop, 155.
58. Ibid, 157.
59. Meagher, 74.
60. Ibid, 75.

V

Man On The Run

IN DISCUSSING THE FLIGHT OF LEE HARVEY OSWALD after the assassination of President Kennedy it is important to remember that Oswald expected—and may have desired—to be apprehended.

When he left the Paine residence early on Friday morning, Oswald left behind $170 (nearly all the cash he had) and his wedding ring. Whatever had transpired between him and Marina the evening before, it is clear that he reached for his rifle only after weighing his options.

With a dozen dollars in his pocket, the assassin couldn't hope to get far. He perhaps could have fled Dallas, but then where? He had left his rifle in the Depository, three shells by the window, his clipboard, and his blue jacket. How long could he hide?

The proof of Oswald's own expectation of arrest lies in the route, direction, and methods he chose to travel in the hour after the assassination. Leaving the Book Depository at 12:33 p.m., he proceeded to his rooming house by bus and by taxi.[1] Much has been made of the fact that Oswald walked up Elm Street (into downtown Dallas) to board a bus which would take him back down Elm Street and into Dealey Plaza. The bus, however, was en route to the Oak Cliff section of town where Oswald kept his rented room, so it was the logical route for the assassin to take.

Sylvia Meagher, not satisfied with bus schedules and the destination Oswald apparently had in mind, dryly noted: "For a murderer to return to the scene of the crime is, of course, in the best classical tradition, but isn't a little time supposed to elapse before such a compulsion prevails?"[2]

Readers will remember that Ms. Meagher was unsatisfied because

Oswald managed to retain his composure and walk out of the front entrance to the Depository. She rushes to judgment, apparently, with no consideration for the thought that Oswald, in his state of mind, might have recognized the bus as a sanctuary of sorts, and not really considered the route it might travel en route to his destination.

Oswald left the bus when it became stalled in the heavy traffic that disrupted downtown Dallas immediately following the assassination. Since he had already paid his fare, and ever considerate of the value of money, he asked driver Cecil McWatters for a transfer. That afternoon, the transfer (with McWatters' unique validating stamp) was found in Oswald's shirt pocket.[3] From McWatters' bus near the intersection of Elm and Lamar Streets, Oswald walked southeast about three blocks and got into a taxi at the intersection of Lamar and Commerce Streets.[4] Only eighteen minutes had elapsed since the assassination.

Cab driver William Whaley told his taxi firm on the day after the assassination that he recognized Oswald from a newspaper photograph as a man he had driven to Oak Cliff during the lunch hour the day before.[5] Whaley subsequently identified Oswald as his passenger when the alleged assassin was displayed in a somewhat dubious police line-up.[6] Being in no hurry (Oswald may have thought that the police officers would be waiting for him at his rented room) he offered to give the cab up for an elderly lady who had apparently seen him enter the taxi and desired another for herself. The woman refused the offer, and Oswald asked Whaley to take him to 500 North Beckley.[7]

Since his rented room was actually at 1026 North Beckley, I believe that Oswald asked Whaley to deliberately drive past his rooming house in order to make certain that law enforcement officers were not waiting for him. He must have known that he would be missed quickly by his supervisor at the Depository, and that some witnesses in Dealey Plaza had seen him in the sixth floor window. As we'll see, both estimates were correct.

Whaley dropped Oswald off at the intersection of Beckley and Neely Street about 12:54 p.m. Various critics have maintained that Whaley could not have made the trip across the Houston Street viaduct and into Oak Cliff in six minutes. Most don't mention that Whaley had been driving a cab in Dallas for more than three decades. If anyone knows how to time lights and cut corners, it's a cab driver with experience under his belt. Subsequently, Whaley displayed to investigators that he could cut two minutes from the best time police officers could drive the route.[8]

Since Oswald departed the taxi in the 700 block of North Beckley, he had but three blocks to walk back to his rented room. Based on my own walks through the site, the stroll took him about five minutes. He arrived at 1026 North Beckley at a minute before one o'clock. The boarding house was owned by Mr. and Mrs. A.C. Johnson. The Johnsons employed a housekeeper, Mrs. Earlene Roberts, who recalled Oswald arriving after she had turned on the television to watch coverage of the assassination.[9] Oswald didn't respond when she glanced at him as he walked in, and called, "Oh, you are in a hurry!"[10] Oswald went to his room and stayed for three or four minutes, then left the boarding house. He had zipped on a jacket and concealed his pistol in the waistband of his slacks.[11]

Carrying a concealed weapon is a crime. This must have been a fact unknown to Sylvia Meagher, since she made no mention of the pistol Oswald picked up while at his rented room. Indeed there is no mention of the pistol at all until Ms. Meagher launches into a discussion of the ballistics identification of the bullets that killed Officer Tippit.[12]*

Ms. Meagher is not alone in ignoring the concealed pistol. Most critics never bother to mention that carrying a hidden handgun is a crime. Perhaps they engage in the practice on a daily basis themselves and thus find nothing unusual in the fact that, when arrested, Oswald still had the revolver in his possession. But to a normal, everyday citizen, Oswald's actions can be explained in just one way . . . that he anticipated having a need for his pistol, so he brought it with him.

The need for the revolver was to arise very shortly. The Johnson's housekeeper paid little attention to Oswald's departure and when last she saw him, Oswald was standing near a bus stop in front of the boarding house, on the same side of Beckley Avenue.[13]

Meanwhile, back at the Depository, the description of the assassin

---

* *The revolver isn't even listed in the* Accessories After the Fact *index. Perhaps Ms. Megher believed that by ignoring the pistol, she could maintain her fantasy that Oswald was "totally innocent of the assassination and had no foreknowledge of it."* [14]

had been broadcast. Fifteen-year-old Amos Euins, who had seen the gunman take aim and fire from the sixth floor window, told Sergeant D.V. Harkness and television reporter James Underwood that the shots had come from the building. *Dallas Times Herald* staff photographer Bob Jackson had seen the rifle being withdrawn from the window.

But the Warren Commission's star witness (and the only one who identified the gunman in the Depository window as Lee Oswald) was forty-five-year-old Howard Brennan. He watched spellbound as the gunman fired the final shot and then disappeared from view. Minutes after the assassination, he described the suspect as white, slender, weighing about 165 pounds, about 5'10" tall and in his early thirties.[15] Doubtless Brennan's description led to a police broadcast in which the suspect was described.[16]

Three Depository employees were kneeling in the southeast corner of the fifth floor when the shots were fired. Brennan recognized Harold Norman and James Jarman, Jr., when they left the building moments after the shooting. The third man was Bonnie Ray Williams. All three men told investigators that they had heard shots fired directly above their heads.[17] Norman, in fact, told officers that he heard shells being ejected on the floor above.

In the Oak Cliff section of Dallas, Officer J.D. Tippit doubtless heard the description of the President's assassin as it was broadcast over channel one of the police radio at 12:45 p.m.[18] The description matched the one Howard Brennan had given officers outside the Depository. Tippit may have heard it again three minutes after the first broadcast, and then again eight minutes later.[19] Had he been listening to channel two (unlikely since he communicated with the police dispatcher on channel one at about 12:45, he would have heard the same description broadcast at 12:54 p.m.[20]

During the minutes just after 1:00 p.m., Lee Oswald walked from directly in front of his boarding house to the southeast corner of 10th Street and Patton Avenue, some nine-tenths of a mile away.[21] If he walked at a brisk pace, he would have reached the corner seconds after 1:15 p.m.[22]

Officer Tippit, meanwhile, cruising east on 10th Street, passed the intersection of 10th and Patton. Oswald had been walking northeast on

Patton, and was about a hundred feet past the intersection. Tippit pulled to the curb, stopped Oswald, and called him over to his car.[23] Of course, Oswald's general description was similar to the one broadcast over police radio beginning a half-hour before.[24]

Tippit held a brief conversation with the pedestrian, either talking through the rolled-up police car passenger window or the open vent window. Tippit then opened his door and stepped out of the car, walking around toward the front of the vehicle. As he reached the left front wheel, Oswald pulled a revolver and fired several shots.[25]

Four bullets hit Tippit. One plowed into his forehead, and two others ranged through his chest. One punctured the heart and would have been fatal if the head wound had not.[26] The officer fell to the pavement, killed instantly by the gunshots.[27]

At least a dozen witnesses saw the man with the revolver near the Tippit killing site at the time of or just after the shooting. By nightfall on the day of the assassination, five of them had identified Lee Harvey Oswald as the man they saw.[27]

Whatever problems the critics have with the official version of the assassination, the Tippit killing appears academic. Oswald, as we will see, was arrested a half-hour after the crime with the revolver still in hand. The empty shells the gunman cast aside as he fled the killing scene were fired in that revolver.[28] Still, such minor details hold no sway over many writers of books on the assassination.

The reason for this lack of appreciation for damning circumstantial evidence is obvious. As Professor Hugh Trevor-Roper wrote in his introduction to *Rush to Judgment*:

> "The plain fact is that there is no evidence at all to explain how or why the Dallas police instantly pounced on Oswald, and until some adequate explanation is given, no one can be blamed for entertaining the most likely hypothesis: that the Dallas police had undisclosed reasons for arresting Oswald even before they had available evidence pointing towards him. Once that hypothesis is admitted, almost all the evidence accepted by the Commission can be reinterpreted in a different way." [29]

Note how conveniently Professor Travor-Roper ignores the Tippit killing. By doing so, he no longer has to deal with a singular bit of logic—that "once the hypothesis is admitted" that Oswald killed

Tippit, there can be little doubt that he killed the President as well. The critics face an impossible task: to prove Oswald innocent of the assassination, they must prove him innocent of the Tippit murder as well.

To do so, critics attempt to destroy the eyewitness testimony that placed Oswald at the crime scene and described his flight from it. Mark Lane, for example, sought to confuse witness Helen Markham and deliberately led her to describe Tippit's killer as someone other than the man she saw.[30] Since this book is concerned with the assassination, and because I believe physical evidence against Oswald in the Tippit killing is conclusive, I will but mention the eyewitness accounts. But let me discuss in detail one witness the critics seldom bring forth: Johnny Calvin Brewer. The young man appears not at all in *Rush to Judgment*. Meagher gives him less than half-a-page,[31] Weisberg only passing notice. Yet Brewer is the sole, unsensational explanation of how the Dallas Police quickly pounced on Oswald.

Brewer comes into view only as Oswald headed, on foot, for the Texas Theater, located some eight blocks from the scene of the Tippit shooting.[32] It is several blocks removed from the point along Jefferson Boulevard where several witnesses last saw Oswald running.[33] As one might expect, since Jefferson is a major thoroughfare, police sirens sounded there just after Tippit was found dead.

Johnny Brewer was one of the individuals along the Boulevard who heard the sirens.[34] Brewer was manager of Hardy's Shoestore, located a few doors east of the Texas Theater.[35] He heard the radio broadcasts about the assassination and the killing of Officer Tippit.[36] When he heard sirens, Brewer "looked up and saw a man enter the lobby."[37] The store's lobby was a recessed area measuring some fifteen feet between the sidewalk and the store front. As Brewer watched, a police car on Jefferson made a U-turn, and the sirens grew fainter as cars raced away. Brewer watched the man in his lobby look over his shoulder and turn around, then walk up West Jefferson toward the Texas Theater. Brewer testified that the man ". . . looked funny to me . . . . His hair was messed up and looked like he had been running, and he looked scared."[38]

Brewer noticed that the man wore a T-shirt beneath his outer shirt, and wore no jacket. (The Tippit killer had, in fact, discarded his jacket during his flight. The garment was found some blocks from the killing site.)[39] Brewer left his shoestore and followed the man up Jefferson, then watched as he ducked around the cashier and into the Texas Theater. The cashier, Julia Postal, saw the man as he entered the lobby, but paid him no attention as she stepped from her booth out into the street, attracted there by the sounds of police sirens.[40]

Brewer asked Mrs. Postal if the man they had seen had stopped to buy a ticket. She replied, "No, by golly, he didn't!" When she and Brewer turned around to look for the man, he had disappeared into the theater.[41]

Sending Brewer into the theater to look for the man he'd followed, Mrs. Postal called the police. At 1:45 p.m., police radio dispatchers confirmed that they had received information that the suspect in the Tippit killing just went into the Texas Theater.[42] Patrol cars carrying more than a dozen officers converged on the theater.[43] Patrolman M.N. McDonald and three other officers entered the theater from the back entrance.[44] Other officers entered from the front, and began searching the balcony area.[45] Detective Paul Bentley ran to the projection booth and told the projectionist to turn up the house lights.

Johnny Brewer met Officer McDonald and the other policemen at the alley door, then stepped onto the stage with them and pointed out the man who had entered the theater without buying a ticket. The suspect was seated alone at the back of the theater's main floor near the right center aisle. He was Lee Harvey Oswald.[46]

Another half-dozen patrons were on the main floor and about the same number up in the balcony. Officer McDonald proceeded to search two men in the center of the main floor. He then walked up the right center aisle to the row where Oswald sat waiting. Stopping abruptly, McDonald told Oswald to stand. Oswald got up, then brought up both hands.[47] As McDonald reached to search Oswald's waist for a gun, he heard Oswald mutter, "Well, it's all over now."[48]

Oswald then reached for his pistol with his right hand; he punched McDonald between the eyes with his left. Keep in mind that critics will have you believe that this is behavior characteristic of a man who is innocent of any wrongdoing.

McDonald cocked his right fist and hit Oswald back, using his left hand to grab at the revolver. Both men fell into the theater seats.[49] A trio of other officers made their way toward the fist fight and grabbed Oswald from the front, rear, and right side. McDonald, falling into the seats with his left hand on Oswald's revolver, felt something graze across the heel of his hand and heard what sounded like the snap of the pistol's hammer hitting a cartridge casing.[50] He felt the pistol scratch his cheek as he pulled it from Oswald's grasp.[51] Detective Bob Carroll grabbed the gun from McDonald.[52] Johnny Brewer testified that during the brief fist fight, he heard one of the officers exclaim, "Kill the President, will you?"[53] The Warren Commission correctly concluded that it was highly unlikely that Brewer heard such a remark, since the officers were pursuing Oswald for Tippit's murder. This single quote has been blown completely out of proportion by assassination sensationalists, since officers could not have possibly connected Oswald with the assassination at the time they arrested him (unless the entire affair had been carefully staged). I suggest that what Brewer really heard was another officer saying, "Kill a policeman, will you?"

Robert Sam Anson, in *They've Killed the President!*, couldn't leave well enough alone. In his over-reaching attempt to cast suspicion on anyone connected with the case, Anson wrote:

> *"Now the other officers were swarming over Oswald, punching and grabbing him. 'Kill the President, will you,' one of them shouted as Oswald went down beneath his seat . . . . The police had their man. As they led him away the man in the front row who had fingered him rose from his seat, walked outside and quietly disappeared."*[54]

You and I know that there was no "man in the front row," only Johnny Calvin Brewer. Anson conveniently leaves Brewer out of the picture—no pun intended.

And in what, in my opinion, deserves to rank as a tremendous feat in the art of conclusion jumping, Robert Groden asserts that Oswald was running into the theater on purpose, and not just to hide: "To Oswald, who may have gone to the Texas Theater to meet his FBI contact—a most logical meeting between informant and 'control'—it must have been clear the cops had come to shoot first and ask questions later."[55] * [FOOTNOTE NEXT PAGE]

Veteran critic Harold Weisberg, who apparently disbelieves everything about the Warren Report except the page numbers and copyright date, chose the Dallas Police as his target:

> *"What is proper police procedure on approaching a dangerous killer who had accommodated the arresting officer by raising his hands in surrender? Dallas-style, the policeman does not order the suspect to move . . . the policeman just grabs the surrendering suspect and starts a fight."* **

Since when does a "dangerous killer" accommodate officers by surrendering? Since when does a suspect who raises his hands "in surrender" bring a fully-loaded revolver up with them? Had I been McDonald, I would have been hard-pressed not to draw on Oswald in self-defense. Apparently, Weisberg would rather a second policeman had died rather than involve Oswald in a struggle in which he might justifiably have been hurt.

Oswald, struggling and screaming about police brutality, was quickly led out of the theater's front entrance. Already a crowd had gathered there, and as the suspect was taken to a police car, some of the more vocal members of the group demanded Oswald be killed.

At 1:51 p.m., the officers in car 2 reported on their radio that they were on their way to headquarters with their suspect.[57]

It was a day for coincidences. At 2:15 p.m., Police Captain Will Fritz returned to the homicide and robbery bureau's office, saw two detectives standing there with Sergeant Gerald Hill, and asked the men to go get a search warrant. Fritz directed the men to the Fifth Street address in Irving where they might find a missing Depository employee, not knowing Hill had just returned from the Texas Theater with Oswald in tow. At the mention of Oswald's name, Hill said, "Captain, we will save you a trip." Pointing to Oswald he said, "There he sits."[58]

Evidence against Oswald in the Tippit murder is overwhelming. The killer had ejected cartridge cases from his pistol as he ran from the scene. Those cases had been fired in the handgun Oswald possessed at the time of his arrest. One firearms expert positively identified one of

---

* *I consider Groden's first book to be characterized by ample speculation and lacking attribution. His second book,* High Treason, *at least contains footnotes.*[56]

** *To be charitable, it was Weisburg's first book* Whitewash, *page 60. As a former Dallas resident, I'm ignoring his comments about my city of residence.*

the bullets from Tippit's body as having been fired from Oswald's pistol.[59]

It seems quite natural to assume that most critics would ignore Illinois police expert Joseph D. Nicol and his opinion regarding the bullet recovered from Tippit's body. And all the critics do ignore him with the exception that he is mentioned in *Rush to Judgment*. Here, Mark Lane seeks to invalidate Nicol's conclusions by insinuating that he was biased against Oswald and insisting that someone who believed the accused assassin innocent should have been appointed to study the bullet as well.[60]*

David Belin, who served as assistant counsel to the Warren Commission, wrote in *November 22, 1963—You Are The Jury* that: "Thus, we have the scientific evidence that unequivocally showed that Lee Harvey Oswald killed Officer J. D. Tippit. Even had there been no eyewitnesses to the Tippit shooting, the apprehension of Oswald less than forty-five minutes after the murder with the murder weapon in his possession was certainly strong evidence that Oswald was the killer. And when you add to this evidence the actions of Oswald in the theater in taking out his gun and resisting arrest and the actions of Oswald before he went into the theater that aroused the suspicion of Johnny Calvin Brewer, the case against Oswald becomes exceedingly strong."

Belin then, as if he needed their help, invokes the aid of eyewitness testimony in the Tippit killing:

> *"And when you add to all of this the positive identification by the six eyewitnesses who were taken to the Dallas Police Department: W.W. Scoggins, who saw Oswald pass within twelve feet of his cab; Ted Callaway and Sam Guinyard, who saw Oswald running from the scene with gun in hand; Helen Markham, who saw the murder from across the street; and Barbara Jeanette Davis and Virginia Davis, who saw Oswald cut across the front yard of their house–there could be no reasonable doubt that the murderer of Dallas Police Officer J. D. Tippit was Lee Harvey Oswald."*[61]

Counsel Joe Ball put it plainly when he said that in all his courtroom experience, he had "never seen a more 'open and shut case.'"[62]

Oswald was questioned for some twelve hours during the week-

---

* Nicol is mentioned in Meagher's book, but in connection with identification of a bullet related to the assassination.

end of the assassination.[63] Throughout the questioning, he denied any involvement with the assassination and the murder of Officer Tippit. No notes or tape recordings were apparently kept of Oswald's questioning.[64] Why Police Captain Fritz chose not to maintain a record of the interrogations is a matter of continuing controversy. It is safe to say, though, that Oswald lied about substantial and incriminating evidence which would have linked him with both killings.

Oswald lied about owning a rifle. Captain Fritz confronted his prisoner with evidence that Oswald had ordered the rifle under an assumed name. Oswald denied the claim.[65] When police displayed photos that showed Oswald with both a rifle and a pistol, Oswald charged that the pictures were fakes aimed at incriminating him.[66] The photos had apparently been taken by Marina with Oswald's Imperial Reflex camera.*

When he was first questioned, Oswald claimed that the only thing he'd done wrong was to carry a gun and resist arrest.[67] Captain Fritz asked Oswald why he was carrying the pistol, and the young man answered, "Well, you know about a pistol. I just carried it."[68] Oswald told officers he had purchased the handgun in Fort Worth, when, in fact, he'd ordered the revolver from a mail order business in Los Angeles.[69]

Oswald further denied using the aliases "Alex J. Hidell" and "O. H. Lee." In his billfold was a forged selective service card bearing his photo and the name Hidell. Oswald told Fritz that he knew no one named Hidell, that he had never received a package at his post office box addressed to Hidell, and that his landlady misunderstood his name and thus he was registered at the boarding house as "O. H. Lee."[70] Of course, Oswald declined to mention that he had signed the register himself as "O. H. Lee."[71]

Oswald told the officers that Wes Frazier and his sister were both mistaken about the long package Oswald had carried in Frazier's car that morning. Oswald told Fritz that the only sack he had carried to work was a lunch sack.[72] Indeed, the accused assassin told Fritz that he was eating lunch at the time of the assassination.[73]

Oswald further stated that he left the Depository because foreman

---

Critics make the same charge today, apparently without justification. HSCA investigators found the photos genuine.

Bill Shelley had told him there would be no further work that day. Shelley denied seeing Oswald at any time after the assassination.[74]

FBI Special Agent James Bookhout, who represented the Bureau at most of the Oswald questioning sessions, summed up the attitude of the prisoner: "I think you might say anytime that you asked a question that would be pertinent to the investigation, that would be the type of question he (Oswald) would refuse to discuss."[75] Admittedly, the number of investigators who crowded into the third floor interrogation room made it difficult for officers to gain Oswald's confidence and encourage him to tell the truth.[76] Police Chief Jesse Curry said later that he and his staff had literally violated every principle of interrogation.[77]

The shouts and bedlam of the hundreds of reporters from all around the world added to the oppressive atmosphere in the interrogation room. The most prudent step Curry could have taken was to bar the press from the building. But Curry chose instead to accommodate the press. That decision proved not to be his undoing, but that of his prisoner. As we shall see, it was all too easy for Jack Ruby to slip into the police department basement two days after Oswald's arrest and exact his revenge on the assassin.

1. WCR, 147.
2. Meagher, 74.
3. WCR, 147.
4. Ibid., 152.
5. Ibid., 151.
6. Ibid.
7. Ibid., 152.
8. Belin, 416.
9. WCR, 154.
10. Ibid.
11. Ibid., 155, 168.
12. Meagher, 280.
13.WCR, 154.
14. Letter to the Author, June 19, 1977.
15. WCR, 133.
16. Ibid.
17. Ibid., 79
18. Ibid., 155.
19. Ibid.
20. Ibid.
21. Ibid., 154.
22. Ibid.
23. Ibid., 155.
24. Ibid.
25. Ibid.
26. Lattimer, 311.
27. WCR, 155.
28. Lattimer, 311.
29. Lane, 13.
30. Roberts,72.
31. Meagher, 87.
32. WCR, 164.
33. Ibid.
34. Ibid., 165.
35. Ibid., 164.
36. Ibid., 165.
37. Ibid.
38. Ibid.
39. Ibid.
40. Ibid.
41. Ibid.
42. Ibid.
43. Ibid.
44. Ibid.
45. Ibid.
46. Ibid.
47. Ibid.
48. Ibid.
49. Ibid., 166.
50. Ibid.
51. Ibid.
52. Ibid.
53. Ibid.
54. Anson, 38.
55. Groden and Model, 277.

56. *High Treason* co-authored with Harrison Livingston.
57. WCR, 167.
58. Ibid.
59. Ibid., 161.
60. Lane, Op Cit, Page 167.
61. Belin, 112.
62. Ibid.
63. WCR, 167.
64. Ibid.
65. Ibid.
66. Ibid., 168.
67. Ibid.
68. Ibid.
69. Ibid.
70. Ibid., 169.
71. Ibid.
72. Ibid.
73. Ibid.
74. Ibid., 170.
75. Ibid., 188.
76. Ibid.
77. Ibid.

VI

The Madness Begins

NINETEEN HUNDRED SIXTY-SIX WAS A BANNER YEAR for critics of the Warren Commission Report. No fewer than five books—Mark Lane's *Rush to Judgment*, Richard Popkin's *The Second Oswald*, Frenchman Leo Sauvage's *The Oswald Affair*, Harold Weisberg's *Whitewash*, and Jay Epstein's *Inquest* all hit the bookstores, as critics swarmed like a group of hungry vultures descending upon the helpless Commission and its work.

Also appearing that year was a slim volume that marked the beginning of an obsession for Midlothian, Texas, newspaper publisher Penn Jones. Jones' first book, *Forgive My Grief*, was followed in succeeding years by three additional volumes that added to the basic premise of the initial book.

Two years earlier, Thomas Buchanan, a former *Washington Evening Star* reporter,[1] produced the first major work to raise questions about the assassination. *Who Killed Kennedy?* was subjected to scathing attacks in reviews and newspaper columns.

In producing their texts, Lane and Epstein in particular had set the literary world on its ear. Norman Mailer reviewed *Rush to Judgment*, proclaiming that he was impressed no end by the "somewhat staggering facts" the book contained.[2] Indeed Mailer waxed lyrical about Lane's work, and sought to display his knowledge of recent American history as well when he wrote: "If one tenth of them (the facts in Lane's book) should prove to be significant, then the work of the Warren Commission will be judged by history to be a scandal worse than the Teapot Dome."[3]*

---

* *Years later, my writing instructor in college, a comrade of Mailer's during World War II, criticized my involvement with the assassination controversy and advised me that I was steering myself down a "pathway*

If I were given a thousand dollars for each reviewer who had read not only the critics' books, but the Warren Report and the twenty-six volumes of exhibits and testimony as well, I would not have enough cash to make a down payment on a second-hand Volkswagen.

From the nearly eighteen thousand pages that comprise the twenty-six volumes, almost any author can select nearly any quote to prove literally any given point. The critics have done just that. From the Watergate burglars to zombie CIA agents, they've been able to make the public believe that almost everyone within the Dallas city limits that Friday had a hand in the assassination of President Kennedy.

Other reviewers were similarly infected by the same malady which gripped Mailer. Alistair Cooke wrote that Lane had "destroyed beyond a reasonable doubt the whole theory of a single assassin."[4] In writing of Epstein's work, Richard N. Goodwin attested that "the limits of my knowledge prevent any final assessment" of *Inquest*, and, to no one's surprise, said he found the book "fascinating."[5]

Reviewing these books critical of the Warren Report should have been a task given to street-smart investigative reporters. Allowing literary critics to digest and comment upon works like *Rush to Judgment* and *Inquest* was tantamount to allowing the society editor to cover a street riot.

But the real problem lay not in the reviews themselves. Literally millions of Americans read only the reviews, to the exclusion of the Report, the volumes, and the critics' books. Where once the Warren Commission had put forth the truth and was believed, now the doubts of the critics caused doubt in the public mind. And the doubt held sway. Indeed, as Charles Roberts noted, the decline of confidence in the United States government, an inarguable consequence of books like Lane's, may itself prove to be "judged by history to be a scandal worse than the Teapot Dome."[6]

The harm didn't stop with erosion of public confidence. Recently it extended to the colossal waste of taxpayers' money. In 1979, the House Select Committee on Assassinations spent six million dollars to

---

to hell" just like his "buddy, Norman." Mailer, for his part, observed the tenth anniversary of Kennedy's death by telling listeners at a "Committee to Investigate Assassinations" conference to beware a storm of excrement that was bound to descend.

conclude that Oswald had fired the shots which killed Kennedy and Tippit. I'll discuss the HSCA's tangled effort later in this book.

I also agree with Roberts that the real question which must be asked of the critics is not one regarding their "new evidence." They haven't any. The real question is how people like Lane, Meagher, Weisberg, Thompson and others could spend their time examining the same source material that the Warren Commission relied upon, yet arrive at an opposite conclusion. Mark Lane once labeled the Warren Commission a group of men "blinded by the fear of what they might see."[7] I believe that the same sentiment holds true for the critics, who are blinded by the fear that the assassination was no more than they were told it was, the crazed act of a single man.

The question is, why do the critics fear such a simple explanation? The answer is three-fold. Some simply wish to make money. Others desire to embody the President's assassination with political significance it clearly lacked if Oswald were the lone assassin. Third, some seek to score other, more personal political points, such as blaming a conservative establishment for an end to the reforms of a fairly liberal Kennedy. More recently, a new generation of critics has joined the old. Propelled by the belief that all the nation's ills stem from that day twenty-seven years ago when Kennedy was killed, these new critics have left virtually no stone unturned in their misguided efforts to tell you and me what really happened when "they" killed the President. These are represented in part by Robert Groden, Henry Hurt, Howard Roffman, Anthony Summers, Larry Harris, Gary Shaw, and David Scheim.

The dubious "rocks" these latter-day critics have "turned over" for us include the following: forgery of the President's autopsy x-rays and photographs, "assassins" caught forever on film taken by assassination spectators, organized crime planning the hit on President Kennedy, alteration of the President's body sometime before the autopsy was performed, a mental patient who confessed to being part of a team of gunmen in Dealey Plaza, and Lyndon Johnson being involved in the plot to kill his predecessor.

All this adds up to speculation and innuendo. The critics are awfully good at asking questions, but woefully short when it comes time to provide answers. As we will see later in this book, most of their arguments tumble down when confronted by the one thing in this case that won't change: the physical evidence.

Dr. John K. Lattimer, who wrote *Kennedy and Lincoln,* has called the critics "professional contrarians, who will say or support anything, as long as it is lurid."[8] The description is by far the most apt I've seen.

So who are these "contrarians," and what do they have to say? All told, there are a baker's dozen who warrant closer examination, if for no other reason than the fact that their books have reached some semblance of wide distribution.

The grandfather of the modern-day critics was a man few of them will acknowledge today, so irresponsible were his speculations on the assassination. He was Thomas Buchanan, an expatriate living in Europe in 1964. Buchanan's book, *Who Killed Kennedy?,* was published before the Warren Report was even issued. Apparently Buchanan became the first in a long line of critics determined not to let the grass grow under his feet.

Buchanan spoke luridly of shots from the triple underpass; a sentiment later favored by Mark Lane, in the days before the grassy knoll arose as the prime suspect, and before critics had bothered to come to Dallas and see for themselves that persons firing at the President from the underpass would have no way to conceal themselves. Lane was the first critic to shift the location of the second gunman. The fact that he relied on the assertions of Buchanan in the first place must make one pause and consider the value of his work.

Buchanan's thesis was simple, albeit unprovable. He wrote that a mysterious Texas oilman, a "Mr. X," had masterminded the assassination in order to protect the depletion allowance. This was heady stuff, made all the more implausible by a German named Joachim Joesten. Joesten, to his credit, was a concentration camp survivor who had been interred by the Gestapo after the Nazis found him "politically unreliable."[9] He added much to Buchanan's theories, lengthening the list of assassins by including the FBI, the CIA, and the United States Army. Indeed, Joesten's first book, *Oswald—Assassin or Fall Guy?,* was published in the United States within weeks of Buchanan's work. The author is to be credited with fostering much of the pro-conspiracy sentiment that exists in Europe today.

With the issuance of the Warren Commission Report in the fall of 1964, the general public was placated for a moment. Here, with a million copies sold in the first ten days, were all the answers to those trouble-makers asking impertinent questions. Literally every major review of the Report lauded it as a monumental contribution to the truth about the assassination. Years later, many reviewers seemed to suffer from a lapse of memory. Forgetting that they had initially embraced the Report and its conclusions, they rushed into print condemning the Commission's work, leading one to believe that, at best, they had only read the books written by the critics or, more probably, magazine articles based on those books.

The turn-around award certainly goes to *The New Republic* reviewer Murray Kempton, who said in October 1964 that "The Warren Commission has given us an immense and almost indisputable statement for the prosecution."[10] Fair enough. Two years later, in his introduction to *The Second Oswald* by Richard Popkin, a reborn Murray Kempton wrote, "There was never any substantial reason to congratulate the Warren Commission for its performance."[11]

By 1967, most major reviewers and several noteworthy news reporters were accepting the critics at face value. Gone were the cardinal rules of reporting that I learned in radio some years ago—namely, to find out something about the individual who is the source of this new information and then to probe a little deeper in an effort to discover his angle or why he was doing what he was doing.

Much of this get-the-details-later attitude manifested itself after the public embraced Mark Lane's book, *Rush to Judgment*. Deeply flawed and heavily biased, it nonetheless hit the *New York Times* best-seller list and resided there for six full months, spending much of its tenure in the number one slot.[12] By late 1966, even the most unfavorable reviewers of the critics' fiction were giving themselves pause to reconsider.

For his part, Mark Lane had literally become a professional troublemaker.[13] A self-styled liberal, Lane had been a member of the New York legislature, and, it's fair to say, had made that body wish he had never been elected. To pop writer Robert Sam Anson, Lane confided that it was he who had delved into the state funded bomb shelter project (then a matter of personal interest to Nelson Rockefeller) and had come up with questions involving a potential conflict of interest on behalf of several notable politicians.[14]

Doubtless Lane's legislative colleagues breathed a sigh of relief when he retired from state government in 1960.[15] But the liberal blood still boiled in Lane; he began to pursue civil rights work. At the time of the assassination, Lane was headed for a courtroom. Late that afternoon, on the courthouse steps, he encountered an old trial judge who asked Lane if he thought Oswald, acting alone, had killed the President.[16]

That chance conversation gave Lane his break into the big-time world of professional rabble-rousing. Within weeks he was in Dallas, visiting with the dead assassin's mother. His next call was on *Newsweek's* Hugh Aynesworth, who had witnessed not only the assassination and the arrest of Oswald, but Oswald's murder by Jack Ruby as well. "I just left Mrs. Oswald," Lane told Aynesworth, "I think she's going to be a great help to me."[17] He told Aynesworth that he might take Mrs. Oswald to New York and stage a sort of "Town Hall" meeting.[18] She was to tell the gathering there that her dead son was actually an agent of the FBI and CIA. Aynesworth asked Lane, "Was he?" "No, of course not," Lane replied. "I don't think so, but she's trying to make her son look as good as she can. I told her he still didn't look too good. But plenty of people want to hear what she thinks and this should draw a big crowd. I'll have to control her, though. She's going to get troublesome with some of her crazy theories."[19]

In Aynesworth's possession that day were copies of investigative depositions that Lane had obviously not seen.[20] Aynesworth brought forth some of the documents to show Lane, noting that Lane "almost drooled."[21] Lane begged Aynesworth to lend him some of the documents, and Aynesworth agreed, on the condition that Lane would not publicly discuss or release them.[22]

Lane asked Aynesworth to record his thoughts on tape, a practice that he would cultivate in years to come. Aynesworth refused, saying that his thoughts were "incomplete."[23] In the months to come, that same excuse wouldn't wash with Lane. He would record and excerpt interviews with witnesses, whether they were prepared or not.

Next Aynesworth heard, Lane had traveled to Europe, using the documents Aynesworth loaned him to make "wild charges"[24] that Oswald had been "framed" and misquoting assassination witnesses. Aynesworth says he watched the situation with amazement and remorse: amazement that Lane would break his word and steal Aynesworth's materials for Lane's own publicity and financial gain, and remorse that Aynesworth helped Lane get started.[25] As a final installment to the story, Lane noted that the Warren Commission had "buried" one of the documents Aynesworth possessed in Volume 24 of its exhibits and testimony, so he was publishing it as an appendix to *Rush to Judgment*, so as to make the record more nearly perfect."[26]*

Lane's book sold more than 150,000 copies in hardback, then went into paper. Not bad for a criminal lawyer who used to specialize in narcotics cases,[27] had been reprimanded by the New York State Assembly, [28] fined more than $400 for ignoring traffic tickets in Manhattan,[29] and was arrested for disturbing the peace in Jackson, Mississippi.[30] Indeed, Mark Lane appeared to have found his niche.

Possessed of a good sense of self-promotion, Lane rented office space on Fifth Avenue in lower Manhattan and started an organization he called the Citizens Commission of Inquiry (CCI). While the CCI operated for some time prior to the publication of Lane's book, it soon ceased to exist. Actually, one might concede that it had never existed anyway, since most "chapters" were composed of single individuals who had happened to write in for information on the assassination.[31]

Lane had even sought to turn the Warren Commission into an adversary proceeding. Retained briefly by Oswald's mother, he sought to represent the dead assassin as a defense counsel. Although he testified before the Commission twice, both times trumping up evidence to show that Oswald was being railroaded, the panel wisely denied him the limelight. [32]

In July 1966, flushed with the initial success of *Rush to Judgment*, Lane collaborated with film producer Emile de Antonio to produce a film and record version of the book. Here Lane stepped into quicksand.

---

* *Lane's gratitude to Aynesworth is no doubt manifested by a fleeting mention in Lane's other book,* A Citizen's Dissent, *and by two brief mentions in* Rush to Judgment.

He offered Warren Commission counsel David Belin, one of the most outspoken defenders of the Report, the opportunity to view a pre-release copy of the film, and then to rebut the film's content on-camera with the understanding that anything Belin said would be used intact in the film itself. [33]

Belin wrote ten letters to Lane in an effort to accept the offer. The first eight went unanswered. [34] Emile de Antonio did send Belin a postcard after Belin had sent his third letter. On the card, de Antonio mentioned that Lane was in Dallas and would return in two weeks. He also asked Belin to write to Lane at another address. [35] Belin, in *November 22, 1963—You Are the Jury*, notes that: "On one occasion when I learned that Mr. Lane was scheduled to speak in Des Moines, I arranged to have a sheriff serve the letters on Lane. Unfortunately, the speech was canceled." [36]

After Belin's ninth letter, Lane replied and withdrew his offer. His rationale was that since "not a single member of the Commission has agreed to appear in the film and none of the senior counsel have agreed either, we have decided not to settle for bit players." [37]

Whatever Lane's view of Belin's function within the Commission structure, the original offer he and de Antonio made was made to David Belin and no one else. As Belin puts it, the "offer to rebut was unconditional . . . there were no strings attached." [38] It's worth noting that Belin published the text of Lane's original letter in full in his first book. In replying to Lane's withdrawal of the movie offer, Belin wrote: "Your bluff has been called . . . true to form, you tried to hide from the person who could best demolish your fabricated case." [39] Mark Lane's credibility strains to the breaking point when you realize that he called a bit player the man who took the testimony of Howard Brennan, who identified Oswald in the sixth floor window; Roy Truly, Oswald's boss at the Depository; Officer M.L. Baker, who confronted Oswald in the building's lunchroom; Lt. J.C. Day, who processed much of the assassination evidence for the Dallas Police Department; Domingo Benavides and William Scoggins, witnesses to Oswald's flight from the Tippit murder scene, and Johnny Calvin Brewer, who observed Oswald in the shoe store lobby and followed him to the Texas Theater. [40]

Belin notes in his book that while he apparently "won the battle of letters," he lost the war, since the film contains no rebuttal. Belin's parting shot at Lane:

"Although you are certainly entitled to your opinion that I was just a bit player, I would respectfully submit that I am fully qualified as an expert on the facts surrounding the assassination of President Kennedy and the murder of Officer J.D. Tippit.

"Mr. Lane, you have welched on your offer of rebuttal. The reason is obvious: You were afraid . . . afraid of the truth.

"Once again I challenge you, Mark Lane, to thirty minutes on film— that is all I need to demolish your manufactured case." [41]

In 1967 and 1968, Lane backed New Orleans District Attorney Jim Garrison in his abortive and ruinous investigation of the Kennedy assassination.* Other critics steered clear of Garrison. For years following, Lane pursued various other interests, co-authoring a book on the assassination of Martin Luther King with comedian Dick Gregory during the interim. But in March of 1975, Lane re-opened the CCI this time in Washington, D.C.[42] The letter I received from Lane soon afterward was a carefully worded plea for money:

"You can help. You can join with us by becoming a member . . . Your membership dues will help with printing costs, operating costs, and lobbying efforts. We will send you the CCI quarterly newsletter with the information about the assassination and the cover-up that is not available anywhere else." [43]

The letter closed with an appeal to my patriotism:

"Your membership will demonstrate the interest of the American people in knowing once and for all who killed President Kennedy, why he was killed, and why so many powerful forces have for so long hidden the truth from us."[44]

What interest could I demonstrate? I was only sixteen-years-old. I couldn't even vote! I suppose those considerations didn't bother Lane, not as long as I had an allowance.

Lane is apparently unperturbed by the fact that even the reporters and eyewitness he cites have refused to endorse him. Hugh Aynes-

---

* *"Investigation" is a poor choice of words, but there is no other. Critic Harold Weisberg wrote me that "Garrison never really ran an investigation."* [45] *This is one of the few points upon which Weisberg and I agree.*

worth and S.M. Holland are examples. Lane has always insisted that *Rush to Judgment* is not an objective analysis. Truth to tell, Lane has never said whether he believes Oswald innocent or guilty of the assassination. He has stated, numerous times, that if Oswald had been tried, he would not have been convicted.[46]

Soft-spoken, scholarly looking Edward Jay Epstein is outwardly everything Lane is not. Indeed, his ivy-league manner and the fact that he was a Harvard graduate student helped him gain access to the Warren Commission and its staff. *Inquest* began as a master's thesis in government at Cornell.[47] Epstein claims to have interviewed five of the seven commission members and ten of its top staffers, though several, including Francis W. Adams, said they had never talked with the young man.[48]

Assistant Counsel Norman Redlich was interviewed by Epstein. Redlich noted that he had asked Epstein to submit to him, for his approval, any statement Epstein attributed to Redlich. Epstein assured Redlich that, in the interests of accuracy, he would do so. He never did.[49] Redlich wrote that he was "appalled by the inaccuracies" in *Inquest*, and charged that Epstein attributed statements to Redlich which Redlich never made.[50]

The basis for Epstein's book was a study of a government organization, the Warren Commission, and how, in such an unusual situation, it functioned. Like Lane, Epstein cited Commissioners' remarks out of context and rewrote the record to make it appear that the Commission was more interested in protecting organizations like the FBI and the CIA than it was in serving the client of truth. An example is Epstein's treatment of the Warren Commission discussions that grew from hearing of rumors that Oswald was an FBI informer. The Commission traced the rumor to its source, a newspaper reporter. Epstein, looking for some grain of truth that would discredit the Commission, chose not to believe the official explanation and insisted that the Commission sought to discredit the rumor to protect the FBI.

Epstein was also the originator of something *Newsweek* called "The Great Photo Debate."[51] Few loose ends in the assassination case have so fascinated the critics as the disappearance (and subsequent re-surfacing) of the Kennedy autopsy photos and x-rays. In 1966, with the publication of *Inquest*, the autopsy evidence rose to the forefront as a serious issue.

Epstein accepted the FBI's summary report on the assassination without hesitation, since it suited his purpose to believe that governmental agencies would tell the truth in some cases and not tell the truth in others. The FBI report claimed that a bullet had struck President Kennedy in the upper back and had fallen out of the wound, a real feat for a bullet traveling 2,000 feet per second.

Epstein argued that even the Commission's evidence, the President's jacket and shirt, proved that the shot hit Kennedy too low in the back for the bullet to have exited from his throat.* The case could have been settled by a review of the autopsy materials. But the photos and x-rays, some Commission staffers noted, were unavailable.[52]

Epstein then reached his moment of darkest surmise. The official autopsy report may have been rigged, he claimed, in an effort to reinforce the single-gunman theory. Since they were missing or had been misplaced, the x-rays and autopsy photos were the proof of the plot.

As it turns out, they were not missing. Bethesda doctors had given the films to the Secret Service, who had surrendered custody of the material to the Kennedy family. Understandably, the Kennedys withheld the photos and x-rays from view of the public—including the Warren Commissioners—as a matter of taste. For nearly three years, no one pressed the family for the materials.[53]

In the midst of the controversy surrounding the x-rays and photos, generated in no small measure by Epstein's book, two of the autopsy doctors examined the material and stood by what they had told the Warren Commission two years earlier: the wound of entry was in the shoulder, and not the back.[54] The Kennedy family delivered the autopsy x-rays and photos to the National Archives, placing restrictions on viewing and limiting access to recognized experts and Federal investigators.[55]

President Johnson made the comment that he thought it was enough to have the evidence "available to any official body."[56] Clearly,

---

* *The throat exit was essential for the single-bullet theory to have merit. I discuss the theory in a later chapter.*

the President was afraid of the evidence being exploited and used without serving any good or official purpose.[57]

Epstein, for his part, seemed satisfied with the mystery he had created and exploited. He told *Newsweek* that the restrictions on viewing the autopsy materials seemed "very reasonable," and added that, thanks to the autopsy evidence, the possibility of a second assassin would "probably be reduced to nil."[58]

More recently, Epstein has written *Legend: the Secret World of Lee Harvey Oswald*. Published in 1978, this book details the possible relationships Oswald established with the intelligence services of the USSR, the United States, and Cuba. The dust jacket's reverse touts Epstein as the author of *Inquest* and notes, incorrectly, that it was "the book that originally raised questions about the findings of the Warren Commission."[59]

Epstein approaches the assassination from the official viewpoint and maintains Oswald as the only gunman.[60] Most of the book, however, seeks to impress the reader with Epstein's knowledge of the intelligence community, and portions serve their purpose as a detailed Oswald biography. As the FBI noted in answering Epstein's questions about Oswald, the central thesis of *Legend* consists of "apparent speculation" on Epstein's part.[61]

Almost every time the assassination arises as a topic of conversation, someone will make mention of the series of supposedly mysterious deaths that have befallen individuals close and not-so-close to the case. The "mysterious deaths" department is the province of one Penn Jones, Jr., a small town Texas newspaper owner.

Apparently, to the critics, having a connection with the Kennedy assassination is akin to robbing an Egyptian tomb or absconding with the Hope Diamond—a curse will surely follow. The only difference here is that, in the case of the tomb or the diamond, the motive force behind the curse is something other-worldly, while in the case of the assassination, the still-at-large conspirators bring doom upon the witnesses.

Jones argues that "every branch of the government" of the United States "assisted in covering and obfuscating the evidence left after that terrible weekend in Dallas."[62] In closing his first book, *Forgive My Grief*,

Volume I, Jones maintains that "more killings are going to be necessary in order to keep this crime quiet."[63] For that matter, the addition of "Volume I" to the book title would prove unnecessary if the mysterious deaths stopped.

One of the eighteen mysterious deaths Jones trots forth as proof of a plot is that of Earlene Roberts, the housekeeper at the boarding house where Oswald last lived. Mrs. Roberts, a plump widow, was sixty years old, suffered from heart trouble, ulcers and cataracts. Her death made Jones' list with the somewhat familiar remark that "no autopsy was performed."[64] Actually, one was performed at Parkland Hospital. Records there show she died of a heart attack.[65] In his first book, Jones chides the law enforcement agencies for hounding Mrs. Roberts to the grave: "Our information leads us to believe Mrs. Roberts, who suffered from a severe case of diabetes, was badgered by the Dallas Police and had one conviction for driving while intoxicated after she testified before the Commission."[66] Dorothy Kilgallen, the Hearst newspaper columnist, died of an overdose of barbiturates and alcohol in her New York home in November, 1965. Because she had been present at Jack Ruby's murder trial, and had briefly interviewed the accused, she made Jones' list as well.[67] As *Ramparts* magazine noted, "No serious person really believes that the death of Dorothy Kilgallen, the gossip columnist, was related to the Kennedy assassination."[68]

One thing Jones hasn't bothered to explain is why the fringe witnesses are being picked off, rather than those really connected with the crime. Howard Brennan, who saw Oswald fire the fatal shot, lived twenty years after the assassination. I can pick up my telephone and call Oswald's wife. The detective handcuffed to Oswald when the assassin was shot by Jack Ruby, J.R. Leavelle, is a personal friend. Phil Willis, who may have taken the most important photo related to the assassination, is still alive and well. Jack Ruby's brother still makes newspaper headlines here in Dallas.

Indeed, part of Jones' first book is devoted to detailing the contents of a letter he bought from autograph salesman Charles Hamilton. The letter written by Jack Ruby was smuggled out of the Dallas County Jail. As Ruby tells it, a neo-Nazi conspiracy killed the President, and arranged for Ruby, a Jew, to murder Oswald. Ruby's point is that the assassination is actually a Nazi-masterminded front to incite the world to commit another genocide on individuals of the Jewish persuasion.[69] Jones himself has said that the assassination cover-up makes America resemble Nazi Germany back in the 1930s.[70]

In *The Assassination Please Almanac*, Tom Miller writes: "After carefully appraising the strange deaths linked to the Kennedy assassination, the mystery is not so much why all these people were killed, but rather, why they were included on the list in the first place.[71]

As if in postscript, the purveyors of *Executive Action*, Mark Lane and Donald Freed, used the mysterious deaths hokum in both the movie and book of the same title. Listing seventeen "material witnesses," the promotional piece went on to detail with marvelous economy of words, how each met death. It concluded by saying that the *London Sunday Times* had concluded that the odds, on November 22, 1963, against fifteen being dead by February, 1967, were on the order of one-hundred-thousand-trillion to one.[72] The *Sunday Times* later admitted that its actuary was greatly in error.*

Accessories After the Fact author Sylvia Meagher, widely touted by the critics themselves, began her task with a bias equal to that she accuses the Warren Commission of having. While she worked in the field of international public health, the writing of analytical reports was indeed her forté. In *Accessories*, it shows through.

Critics have alleged that Mrs. Meagher spent more time examining the twenty-six volumes of evidence and testimony than any other of their number. From her exhaustive examination, she proceeded to write her book, which has been described as a line-by-line counter to the Warren Report.

While Ms. Meagher's research may have been conspicuous by its scope and detail, her pro-Oswald bias contributed to several important errors, many already cited in this book. She apparently was numbered among the dozens of critics who, despite their pronouncements on the assassination, spent scant time at the scene of the crime. Nonetheless, her book stands today as the critics' bible and her epitaph. Sylvia Meagher died in 1988.

---

* *That didn't stop Lane and Freed from using the actuary in movie ads. An ad from my collection appears in the sixth floor exhibit.*

Maryland poultry farmer Harold Weisberg has weighed into the controversy with a half-dozen heavy hitters, all books in the *Whitewash* series. *Whitewash*, the first book from Weisberg's typewriter,* was self-published in 1965. So basic was the book, covering so much of the ground that sensationalists would plow again and again in years to come, that it probably served as the primer for Jim Garrison's investigation into the assassination.[73]

Readers working their way through *Whitewash* are in for a difficult time. Weisberg's writing is not the clearest. He spends five of his 224 pages detailing the moving of boxes in the southeast and northwest corners of the sixth floor.[74] I have described how the boxes had been moved by officers and reporters during the hours following the assassination. Weisberg, unsatisfied that the boxes had been moved and could not be exactly replaced, claims the official reconstruction of the crime is false.[75]

The second book in Weisberg's series, *Whitewash II*, bore the subtitle *The FBI-Secret Service Cover-Up*. Here, Weisberg attempted to focus, with limited success, on the FBI and Secret Service investigative efforts, the timing of the first shot, and the position of the presidential limousine when Kennedy was first struck.

In *Whitewash II*, Weisberg claimed to be able to discern the exact location of the limousine a moment after the President began reacting to a bullet wound. The famous still photograph taken by James Altgens of the Associated Press does, indeed, show the auto, surrounding buildings and grassways, and the Elm Street road stripes by which Weisberg arrived at his conclusions. His point was that Kennedy had obviously been shot much earlier than investigators indicated, and at a point where much of Oswald's view of the motorcade was blocked by tree branches.[76]

The problem with Weisberg's limousine placement lies in the right-hand margin of the Altgens photograph. The spectators shown waving to the President are also visible in the Zapruder film, taken from the other side of Elm Street. From the Zapruder film, using these spectators as a guide, one can see that the limousine was far enough

---

* Whitewash *literally came from Weisberg's typewriter. Not being able to find a publisher, Weisberg published his typewritten original. The book would have been easier to read had all the keys struck evenly.*

down Elm Street for Kennedy to have been a clear target from the sixth floor window.

In the spring of 1975, I sat in my bedroom-turned-research center and tried to reconcile Weisberg's statements (for which I had great respect) with what I saw in the still and motion pictures. I dashed off one letter to Harold, asking for an explanation of the apparent inconsistencies. I waited two weeks, then wrote another. Ten days later I had my reply:

> *"Dear James,*
>
> *Please try to understand that each thing I do means there is another thing I cannot do, so please do not write to me needlessly because I have been so very busy since September I have not been able to get back to my own writing and in fact have not been able to keep up with day-to-day work.*
>
> *Your April 15 letter fixes on one of my rare mistakes. I can't think of a single mistake I made that did not come from believing something the Commission or one of its staff or the FBI did or said. This is such a case.*
>
> *In the Altgens picture one of the stripes is hidden by the car.**
>
> *My mistake was in believing Liebeler had placed Altgens properly. He did not. Not until it was possible to make a long and detailed study of the Zapruder film in slides was it possible to figure this out. The printed pictures are not as clear."* [77]

How could a sixteen-year-old novice find Altgens in the Zapruder film prints available to him, and a renowned researcher like Weisberg prove unable to locate Altgens with the same materials? Why would an author who accused a Presidential Commission of sloppy ineptitude believe anything the panel produced as evidence? Why did Weisberg not delete the reference to the timing of the first shot from the mass-paperback edition of his book?**

The comments in Weisberg's letter shocked me then and disturb me still. Had he been a little more contrite, admitting that he had made an honest mistake, I would have thought none the worse of him. But an investigator's first responsibility is accuracy. If an error finds its way into print, the least he can do is to admit that he made the mistake and

---

* *The Presidential limousine.*

** *Robert Groden included the road-stripe timing method in* High Treason, *published nearly fifteen years after Weisberg admitted to me that the theory was a compound of error and speculation.* [78]

not try to pawn the responsibility off on someone else.

As you will see, Weisberg still figures prominently in my final solution to the assassination controversy. One portion of his research, detailed in what amounts to *Whitewash III*, a book titled *Photographic Whitewash*, gave me a major piece to the puzzle.

Weisberg's latter day claim to fame among critics has been his enduring ability to pry classified documents out of the National Archives. But even those who think tenderly of him admit that very little new or useful information has been gleaned from the documents that Weisberg has spent years obtaining.*

In another letter, Weisberg encouraged me to spend my available research time with Sylvia Meagher's book, *Accessories After the Fact*. When I happened to mention that I was reading Josiah Thompson's *Six Seconds in Dallas*, Weisberg replied: "Thompson's book is not all that good. What is good in it is plagiarized [sic] from other work. His theorizing is at best dubious."[79] Weisberg's words carry a large measure of truth. The great single contribution made by *Six Seconds in Dallas* to the body of assassination literature was the chart showing the positions of one hundred-ninety witnesses, and a listing of their opinions as to the source, number, and bunching of the shots they heard. The locations chart was an ambitious undertaking, marred, as I've mentioned, by some important and glaring errors.

Obviously, Josiah Thompson and I attach differing weights to eyewitness testimony. Dr. Thompson believes strongly in its validity; I believe that it cannot be relied upon. Oddly enough, Dr. Thompson concludes that the shot which caused Governor Connally's wounds, based on its trajectory, had to have been fired from the Dallas County Records Building, diagonally opposite the Book Depository in Dealey Plaza. Here, he evidently decides that the eyewitness testimony is unreliable. Not one of the one hundred ninety witnesses he cites testified that they believed a shot had been fired from the Records Building. Actually, Dr. Thompson's trajectory analysis is shaky at best; he does

---

* *Weisberg made another error, this one picked up by the* New York Times. *He found an FBI report that inaccurately cited the speed of the Zapruder camera as twenty-four frames per second. Without bothering to check the actual camera, Weisberg rushed the information into print. The camera can't be set to operate at twenty-four frames per second.* [80]

not take into account that the very Zapruder film frames he believes show the hit on Connally also show the Governor leaning backward, thus altering the angle of the bullet through his body. In *After the Assassination*, Dr. John Sparrow wrote that:

> *"The photographs from which Professor Thompson deduces the movements of the President and Governor, when hit, and his assumptions about the effect of the strike of a bullet on the movements of a human body, seem much too uncertain a foundation for the precise calculations that he bases on them."*[81]

In *Six Seconds*, Dr. Thompson postulates that four shots were fired, two from the Depository, one from the Records Building, and one from the grassy knoll. To his credit, though, he refrains from wildly speculating on the conspiracy he believes killed the President. He merely seeks to prove its existence.

Dr. Thompson was a philosophy professor and arranged for a year's leave of absence from the academic world to research and write *Six Seconds*.[82] The success of his book led to his appointment as *Life* magazine's consultant on the Zapruder film. Access to the original film gave him an almost unlimited expertise on what is doubtless the most important single piece of evidence in this case. For years afterward, he peddled that expertise to television talk shows ranging from Geraldo Rivera's *Good Night America* to David Suskind.

The House Select Committee had a good time with Dr. Thompson, dismissing, among other things, his concern about the Carcano bullet casing with the dented lip. HSCA firearms panelists claimed that the casing had been dented upon ejection from Oswald's rifle. In his book, Dr. Thompson mentions that he had thrown literally hundreds of Carcano shells against walls and never dented a single one.[83] To his credit, neither have I. I have, as previously mentioned, created the dent by attempting to re-chamber a fired cartridge casing.

Even Professor Sparrow, in *After the Assassination*, admits that Thompson's strong suit is the wealth of information that he provides in building a case against a single bullet having caused all the non-fatal wounds to Kennedy and Connally. Thompson used the Zapruder film and eyewitness testimony to support his conclusion, rather than belaboring the sound condition of the bullet recovered.

But what Thompson used in *Six Seconds* reflects only what he borrowed from Raymond Marcus, in his short study of the "magic bullet theory" titled *The Bastard Bullet: A Search for Legitimacy for Commission Exhibit 399*. Marcus' little book was published a year before Thompson's.

Thompson believes that bullet 399 can be accounted for as the slug which caused the President's back wound.[84] Implausible as it might seem that a bullet with a muzzle velocity of more than 2,000 feet per second might enter Kennedy's back, penetrate only a short distance, and then fall out onto a stretcher at Parkland Hospital, Thompson faces another problem common to a number of critics.

If the conspirators fired four shots, and bullet 399 and fragments of another that caused the President's head wound were all that were recovered, where did the other bullets go? Did the bullet which wounded Governor Connally—fired from the Records Building, if you believe Thompson—vanish into thin air?* Did another bullet fired from the knoll, according to Thompson, which hit President Kennedy in the head, just disappear, since it doesn't seem to be evident in the autopsy x-rays and photographs?

These are the questions Dr. Thompson has no answers for. Nor can there be any answers, because there were no shots fired from the knoll and the Records Building. But for Thompson to admit that all the shots which hit Kennedy and Connally came from the sixth floor of the Depository, he would also have to admit that his book has suddenly become an exercise in futility.

Instead of offering concrete information, Thompson has, in recent months, taken to making vague pronouncements of a general and suspicious nature. As a spokesman for the critics on the Sixth Floor audio cassette which visitors can purchase as an accompaniment to their tour, Thompson promotes nothing but speculation in calling bullet number 399 "a very curious bullet indeed," and claiming that the Warren Report was intended to show the American people "that the as-

---

* In 1975, gunfire from the Records Building—the second floor this time, not the roof—cropped up in *Appointment in Dallas*. Hugh McDonald, a career law enforcement officer, said that he had obtained a complete confession from the real assassin, who fired (so he said) from a second-floor window in the Records Building. McDonald overlooked one thing. The windows can't be opened in the Records Building. I wrote him and suggested that he visit Dealey Plaza, but he did not reply.

sassination had no more political significance than had Air Force One been struck by lightning."[85]

Encouraged by his foray into the Kennedy assassination controversy, Thompson has become a private investigator. His new book, *Gumshoe*, details his experiences in the espionage-for-pay business.

Whenever a sensational event takes place, there are always people who, for one reason or another, proclaim and manage to convince themselves that they have had previous contact with an individual associated with the well-publicized event. In the Kennedy assassination, several Dallas area residents claimed to have seen Lee Harvey Oswald in the weeks and months preceding the President's death. In many of these cases it is highly unlikely that these individuals had contact with the real Lee Oswald, such as a car salesman who gave Oswald the opportunity to take a test drive when the real Oswald could not drive for instance.

This sort of controversy promoted Richard Popkin, then the Chairman of the Department of Philosophy at the University of California, San Diego, to write a slim volume titled, appropriately enough, *The Second Oswald*. Dr. Popkin's work is brief. It's the only book I've seen which counts the title, copyright, contents and blank pages as actual, numbered pages. Minus its introduction by Murray Kempton, *The Second Oswald* runs to only 101 pages.

"The evidence seems to me compelling," Dr. Popkin wrote, "that there was a second Oswald, that his presence was forced on people's notice and that he played a role on November 22, 1963.[86] Published in 1966, *The Second Oswald* prompted Sylvia Meagher to write that it "is stamped with the authority that can only be achieved by patient and comprehensive study of the testimony and exhibits, an exercise which has been undertaken by lamentably few critics of the Warren Report."[87]

Professor Popkin believes that there were actually two assassins in Dallas when the President was killed; three if you count the "real" Oswald.[88]

Only I don't suppose we can count the "real" Oswald, can we? Dr. Popkin believes that the "real" Oswald's role that day was to act as a decoy and lead police astray, while the "second" Oswald, who was one of the two gunmen, escaped the scene of the crime.[89]

Though Popkin neglects to mention it, most of the appearances of the "second" Oswald were anonymous. The person people saw didn't give his name. Except for a visit to a Mrs. Odio, an anti-Castro Cuban exile (one must remember that the "real" Oswald was pro-Castro) the second Oswald did not express any political affiliations or opinions.[90]

Keeping in mind that the assassination took place late in November, one would have expected the "second" Oswald to have a number of appearances during the preceding month. As Dr. Popkin notes, this was not the case: "In October there seems to have been little double-Oswald activity. This may be explained by the facts that Oswald was looking for a job at the time and that his second daughter was born on October 20."[91]

Now, wait a minute. Why would the activities of the "real" Oswald keep the "second" Oswald from going about his duties as impersonator? Professor Popkin doesn't bother to explain. Popkin, like Lane and other critics, believes Oswald carried curtain rods to work with him on the day of the assassination.[92] And he conveniently avoids discussing the most important half-hour of the real Oswald's life, from just after noon until just after the assassination of President Kennedy.[93]

To Popkin's credit, he at least holds back from accusing the FBI, the CIA, the Secret Service, the Dallas Police, or any other organization of conspiracy to kill the President. But the vagueness of his brief book is its undoing. Armed with an understanding of human psychology, a careful reader will conclude that, aside from a couple of inexplicable events, there just isn't much to *The Second Oswald*.

Credit for lack of speculation can't be given to Leo Sauvage. A writer for *Le Figero*, Sauvage asserted that Kennedy's assassins were representatives of the Dallas Police, coupled with ardent right-wingers and gangsters.[94]

Sauvage's book, *The Oswald Affair: An Examination of the Contradictions and Omissions of the Warren Report*, was published in 1966.[95] The implausibility of Sauvage's conclusion, (gangsters and police working together) speaks for itself.

First-generation critic David Lifton credits his best-selling *Best Evidence* to "insights" that someone had surgically altered the President's body between the time it was removed from Air Force One and its arrival at Bethesda Naval Hospital where the autopsy was performed.

It seems that Lifton, in late October 1966, stumbled across a document written by agents Sibert and O'Neill of the FBI. In the document the two agents mention that when the President's body arrived in the autopsy room, there had been surgery of the head area, namely, in the top of the skull.[96]

In late 1966, Lifton was acting as a devil's advocate in a class on the Warren Commission taught by former Commission attorney Wes Liebeler.[97] You'll recall a mention of Liebeler's name in Chapter Two. It was his disagreement with a crucial section of the Warren Report which caused a delay in publication so that section could be rewritten.

In his class, Liebeler had often challenged Lifton with the same logic I've used with second-generation critics. If there were another assassin, where did the bullet go? In the FBI document, Lifton thought he had found the answer. As he told Liebeler, "They simply took the bullet out, before the autopsy."[98]

Three months later, *Ramparts* magazine published an article written by Lifton and David Welsh, the magazine's new editor. Titled *The Case for Three Assassins*, the piece was a cobbled up version of a rather heady manuscript Lifton had written at the beginning of 1966.[99] The title of Lifton's original work: *Assassination—1963: The Citizen and the Critic: A Dialogue in Defense of Conspiracy.*[100] Fortunately for its readers, *Ramparts* condensed the fifty-page tract into some 30,000 words.

The discovery of the Sibert-O'Neill document turned the conspiracy-minded Lifton onto a random path of adventure and frustration. His mindset originally formed by a Mark Lane lecture, Lifton was soon "playing hardball," talking and arguing with Commission insiders like Liebeler and panel member Allen Dulles.[101]

Lifton's initial research led him, among other things, to stand on Hollywood Boulevard and show the Moorman Polaroid photograph of the assassination to passersby.[102] Mary Moorman was standing next to her friend Jean Hill in Dealey Plaza, and took the picture just as the fatal shot struck the President. In the grainy shadows of the Moorman photo, Lifton thought he had found a gunman atop the grassy knoll.[103] Of course, the fact that he was using a third-generation, greatly enlarged copy of a Polaroid as his point of reference did not matter at all to Lifton.

As we will see, there is no ballistic or medical evidence of a second assassin in this case. None. Undaunted, Lifton seized upon the Sibert-O'Neill report as a means of overcoming the objection he had no answer for. Since he couldn't turn up other bullets from other guns, the next best course of action was to rely upon documents and heresay, then conclude that someone (doubtless a highly placed member of "the conspiracy") had gained access to the President's body, altered the wounds and removed selected bullets or fragments, then put the body back in place at Bethesda so that it could undergo autopsy there.*

It will come as no surprise that Lifton's theory has several problems. First, Kennedy aide Dave Powers denies emphatically that there was ever an opportunity for anyone to seize the President's body. He maintains that Kennedy's coffin was never left unguarded:

> "Lifton's book is the biggest pack of malarkey I ever heard in my life. I never had my hands or eyes off of it (the coffin) during the period he says it was unattended, and when Jackie got up to go to her stateroom . . . we stayed right there with the coffin and never let go of it. In fact, several of us were with it through the whole trip all the way to Bethesda Naval Hospital. It couldn't have happened the way that fellow (Lifton) said. Not even thirty seconds. I never left it. There was a general watch. We organized it."[104]

The thought crossed my mind that Lifton should have talked to Powers prior to publication of his book. Apparently, the same thought never crossed Lifton's mind. Powers could have saved him a great deal of trouble, although the conversation might have cost Lifton plenty. *Best Evidence* stayed on the *New York Times* best-seller lists for three months.** The current paperback edition contains several autopsy photos, publication of which I regard as blatant sensationalism.

Another problem with Lifton's theory concerns the amount of time it might take someone skilled in the art of body reconstruction to alter Kennedy's wounds. Lifton believes that Kennedy's body was shipped in the luggage compartment, presumably in a body bag, separate from the casket. Once in Washington, D. C., the body was taken from the

---

* Sibert and O'Neill apparently got the "surgery" information from an autopsy doctor who was unprepared for the massive head wound Kennedy had suffered. [105]

** Lifton is currently engaged in writing a sequel. [106]

airplane to Walter Reed Army Hospital where the bullets were re-moved, wounds covered up, other wounds created, and the brain taken out.

All this would have to have been done in a hurry—the body was expected back at Bethesda. But suppose that it could have been done as a team effort in, say, thirty minutes. Is such a body reconstruction possible? Forensic pathologists say probably not.

A further problem with Lifton's hypothesis lies in the research he conducted while writing *Best Evidence*. Lifton, like other critics, cate-gorically states that none of the Dallas doctors saw the entry wound in the President's right shoulder.[107] This is crucial to his theory that shots from the front hit the President in the throat and in the head.

The problem with Lifton's assertion is that at least one Dallas doctor, anesthesiologist Marion T. "Pepper" Jenkins, felt the wound. Indeed, Jenkins had corresponded on just this point with Dr. John Lattimer, the author of *Kennedy and Lincoln*. [108]

When *Time* magazine reviewed *Best Evidence* and waxed lyrical about Lifton's work, Lattimer wrote a letter to *Time* in which he stated that Lifton's "evidence" was demonstrably false.[109] He included as proof of his assertion his copies of correspondence with Dr. Jenkins. The letters had been dated well in advance of publication of Lifton's book.*[110]

Lifton responded to Lattimer's letters by accusing him and Dr. Jenkins of pre-dating recent correspondence in an effort to discredit his book![111] Is this the sort of reaction you'd expect from someone who is sure of his facts? Or is Lifton's reaction the kind of thing you'd expect from someone only interested in propounding lurid speculation?

In *Best Evidence*, Lifton notes that in talking with AP photographer James Altgens, he found that a number of people "suddenly appeared" behind the concrete wall to the right of the stairway leading up the slope of the grassy knoll in Dealey Plaza. This was an important discovery for Lifton. One of these individuals spotted by Altgens might be the grassy

---

* Indeed, Lattimer notes in his book that Jenkins knew about the back wound by writing: " . . . (Jenkins) was aware that there was a hole in the back of the President's neck . . . . he could also see a wound of exit on the front of the throat and there was no doubt in his mind that it was the exit wound of the bullet that had entered the back." [112] I discuss these wounds in more detail in a later chapter.

knoll assassin.[113]

Had Lifton bothered to come to Dealey Plaza and investigate, he would have learned that, from an Elm Street perspective, there is no wall on the grassy knoll to get behind. The concrete retaining wall that runs to the right of the stairs runs perpendicular to the street, not parallel to it. An assassin behind the wall would have been in clear view of the three individuals standing on the stairway, and all the eyewitnesses standing across Elm Street.

Lifton charges that the massive head wound suffered by the President was altered before the body was autopsied. How this incredible feat of reconstruction was accomplished is a question Lifton does not address. Remember that he, like most other critics, are in the business of asking questions, not answering them.

Lifton asserts that the head wound was altered because the doctors at Parkland all recall a massive wound at the back of the skull, while the autopsy revealed a wound on the right side.[114] This is an important point of controversy, because it also forms the central argument of Robert Groden's new book, *High Treason*.

The problem with Lifton's thesis is that, aside from Dr. Jenkins, no one examined the President's back. Indeed, including Dr. Jenkins, no one in Dallas turned Kennedy over. It would have been impossible for any of the staff at Parkland to have seen a wound at the rear of the skull. Why do they describe it there?

The answer is a simple one. When Kennedy was brought into the trauma room, he was lying face-up on a stretcher. This is the only position in which the Parkland staff saw him. Thus, to them, the wound at the side of the head would, of necessity, have been at the "back" of the head, since they could see no further than the rearward margin of this wound. The head wound would have been described by the Parkland doctors as being at the back of the head, because the side of the President's head was the most rearward portion of the skull they observed.

The central difficulty Lifton (and Groden) must overcome is the dubious practice of interviewing someone who saw President Kennedy for only twenty minutes—in this case, all the Dallas doctors. And in Lifton's case, the detailed interviews came anywhere from ten to sixteen years after the assassination. For Groden and his co-author Harrison Livingstone, the interviews took place sixteen years or longer after the assassination.

Lifton, like Groden some years later, concludes that the Secret Service was involved in the assassination and the resulting cover-up, including the alteration of the President's body.[115] And the Secret Service involvement, Lifton notes, "is just the beginning."[116] Before we can catch our breath, he notes cryptically that "others had to be involved."[117] Of course Lifton cannot name names and produce evidence. Instead, he calls upon an unnamed organization to undertake a new investigation. Apparently, the investigation concluded just before his book was published did not satisfy him.[118]

Wes Liebeler had warned Lifton, some years before *Best Evidence* was published, about the public skepticism that would greet his theory. "David, I might as well tell you now," Liebeler intoned, "nobody will believe it."[119] Apparently, Liebeler was wrong, but honestly so. The American people may not believe the body-alteration theory, but more important to Lifton, they've certainly bought it.

At best, Lifton's thesis is an effort to overcome two obstacles the critics have faced since the issuance of the Warren Report. If there were a gunman firing at the President from the grassy knoll, where is the medical evidence that a shot hit Kennedy from the front? And, where are the bullets or bullet fragments fired by the second gunman?

Since there is no medical evidence (as we will see) that a shot fired from the front hit either Kennedy or Connally, and since the only bullet and bullet fragments recovered had been fired from Oswald's rifle, speculation and innuendo will only work so long to sell books about the assassination "conspiracy." Sooner or later, there is a need for firm, solid, physical evidence to support the critics' claims.

And when there isn't any physical evidence to fall back upon, the explanation is obvious: it was there—but the conspirators removed it. The fact that they had to alter the President's body to do so is, therefore, a minor (almost given) point. But observe the consequences of this presupposition. Lifton doesn't believe that the back wound existed until the body arrived at Bethesda. The thought of someone firing a shot into the back of the dead President borders on the obscene. None of this appears to bother Lifton. He maintains his theory despite clear evidence to the contrary. The extent of his outlandish charges matters not as long as he and his fellow critics can stay afloat in a sea of speculation.

The best speculator of them all came to national attention first in 1975. That spring, ABC television's Geraldo Rivera hosted three *Goodnight America* programs devoted, at least in part, to the controversy surrounding the Kennedy assassination. As the *piece de resistance* for the first of the three programs, Rivera hosted photo technician Robert Groden who displayed his enhanced version of the Zapruder film. The show marked the first time that the American public had been able to see the film in true motion-picture form.

With comedian Dick Gregory, Groden noted that the President was shot in the throat, from the front, and then made the same claim regarding the very visible head shot. In the film, the President's head moves violently backward after he is struck. This is proof to critics like Groden and Gregory that the shot had exploded in Kennedy's right temple and thrown his body to the left rear.*

A month-and-a-half before his *Goodnight America* appearance, Groden had shown his enhanced Z-film at the Politics of Conspiracy conference held at Boston University. The conclave was sponsored by a group to which I used to belong, the Assassination Information Bureau.[120] Many significant researchers attended the conference. For Robert Groden, the event was so filled with tension and suspicion that he kept his Z-film handcuffed to his wrist.[121]

A year later, Groden joined Peter Model in publishing his first book on the assassination. Titled, *JFK—The Case for Conspiracy*, the work was fraught with fantasy and error. It did however, contain frames from Groden's enhanced film, albeit printed on poor paper, in the wrong order, and reversed.[122] Now, Groden calls the paperback he co-authored "a very important book."[123] Barely twenty-five pages into this "very important book," Groden and Model issue a challenge I just cannot resist. In their words

"at the precise moment of impact (the time of the assassination), Lee Harvey

---

* *This casual observation isn't supported by either theory or evidence, as we will later see. Even critic Robert Cutler called the grassy knoll head shot "shoddy oversimplification."* [124]

> *Oswald . . . was either perched in the southeast corner of the sixth floor,*
> *firing his gun . . . or standing in the doorway of the Depository's main*
> *entrance, watching the motorcade (according to eyewitness and photo-*
> *graphic evidence)."*[125]

No such evidence exists. There is no eyewitness testimony to support the theory that Oswald was standing in the Depository doorway at the time of the assassination. Those who were standing there remember Billy Nolan Lovelady, another employee, as the individual standing just inside the entrance.

The photographic evidence the authors cite is the Altgens photo, the same one Harold Weisberg used to develop his "road-stripe theory." Later in the book, Groden and Model go to great lengths (including using a doctored photograph of Lovelady)* to attempt to prove that the man in the doorway is, in fact, Oswald. The gist of their analysis is that the shirt Lovelady wore on the day of the assassination doesn't seem to be the same as the shirt worn by the man in the Altgens photograph. The man in the doorway, and the shirt he's wearing resemble Oswald as he appeared after his arrest.[126]

Three years later Groden, retained by the House Select Committee as a photographic consultant, wrote the Committee that he had concluded that the man in the doorway was "indeed Mr. Lovelady."[127]

Now, by Groden's own admission, if Oswald weren't in the doorway, where was he? On the sixth floor, firing at the motorcade. Indeed, in his second book, Groden doesn't bring up the "man in the doorway" at all. Nor does he correct the impression that he gave readers of *Case for Conspiracy*, that Oswald was the man in the Altgens photograph.

Groden and Model assert that Oswald, after his arrest, directed police to Mrs. Paine's residence in Irving, where they found among other things photos of Oswald with the rifle and pistol and the negatives of the forged identification cards he carried in his wallet. As we've seen, officers were preparing a search warrant when Oswald was brought to

---

Groden and Model included a still photo from a file taken by assassination spectator John Martin. The HSCA published the same photo in Volume VI of their Appendix to Hearings, *288. The actual photo shows Lovelady with no beard, contrary to Groden's claim. The photo in Groden's book shows Lovelady with a heavy beard.*

the city jail after his arrest. He gave officers no sort of directive.[128]

The clear implication Groden and Model attempt to falsify is that Oswald had nothing to hide. They spend four pages asserting that Oswald's civil rights were violated, an issue having nothing to do with whether or not he shot the President.[129]

Even the photo captions in *Case for Conspiracy* are misleading. The second page of photos published includes three black-and-white views of the southeast corner window from which Oswald fired. The bottom photo was taken on the afternoon of the assassination, with the rifle-rest boxes moved, and the window opened as far as it would go. The assassin had only opened the window halfway, and arranged his boxes to serve as a rest for his elbow and the rifle. This arrangement is evident in my reconstruction of the sniper's nest.

When one re-arranges the boxes, as newsmen did on that afternoon, Oswald's view of the motorcade is blocked, since he only opened the window halfway. Groden and Model draw an imaginary line across the opened window in the photo they depicted, and state:

> *"The bottom photo, taken on the afternoon of Nov. 22 by the late Jack Beers of the* Dallas Morning News, *was snapped from inside the southeast corner 6th-floor window. The window had been raised. However, the dotted line shows the window height at the time of the shooting. Had the sniper rested his gun on the carton (foreground) the telescopic sight would have been blocked by the window sash. Clearly, JFK was not shot from this point."* [130]

The photo Groden and Model cite as evidence proves no such thing. It only shows what we already know, that the boxes were re-arranged after the assassination. Additionally, the photo is flat, and the reader can make no allowance for the different angle at which Oswald aimed his rifle. Groden should know this, since the book touts him as a "multi-media technician specializing in photo-optical image restoration and enhancement."[131]

This impression is heightened by the photo captions on the next page: "With the Dillard and Beers photo proving the impossibility of a gunman's ability to target JFK in a moving limousine . . ."[132] It might interest readers to know that the photos I used to reconstruct the boxes in the window were both taken from street level within seconds of the fatal shot. Tom Dillard's photo, in particular, was of crucial value. When you see the boxes arranged in the Sixth Floor exhibit, they are arranged as they appeared from the street. I've sat on the box in the corner and aimed a long stick out the window. With the window opened halfway, Oswald had no difficulty tracking the President until the auto disappeared under the triple overpass.

Other photos and illustrations in *Case for Conspiracy* purport to show the implausibility of a single bullet hitting both the President and Governor Connally. The drawing Groden and Model chose for the purpose shows Connally seated directly in front of Kennedy in the Presidential limousine.[133] We know from photos taken during the assassination that Connally was seated somewhat to Kennedy's left, and not against the right side of the auto as the drawing depicts. Additionally; as the bullet struck Connally, he was turning to his right, which took his right shoulder even more leftward and into the line of fire. We'll explore the single-bullet theory in detail later in this book.

Groden and Model make much of the fact that the President's brain is missing from the National Archives and has been for some time. The assumption is that Robert Kennedy, for reasons of privacy, either buried or destroyed it. But Groden and Model report that the Archives subsequently located the brain, adding: "Still no independent researcher has been allowed to see what's in the cannister, possibly because of recurring rumors that there might be an 'unidentifiable foreign object' in the brain that could be a spent bullet . . . "[134]

I know of no rediscovery of the brain in the National Archives. The House Select Committee apparently hadn't learned the news either. This is surprising since Groden testified before the HSCA, and had ample opportunity to tell them of the Archives' good fortune. The fact that the brain is unavailable is all too convenient for those who insist it contains hidden "proof."

Preceding David Lifton by about four years, Groden and Model mention the Parkland doctors' description of the massive head wound as further proof of a cover-up. The authors chose to quote Dr. Robert McClelland:

"I was in such a position (at the emergency operating table) that I could very closely examine the head wound, and I noted that the right posterior portion

of the skull had been blasted. It had been shattered, apparently, by the force of the shot so that the parietal bone was protruded up through the scalp and almost along its posterior half as well as some of the occipital being fractured in its lateral half . . . "[135]

Parietal bone, assuming Groden and Model haven't moved it, lies to the side of the skull, and not to the rear. Yet, the gist of *Case for Conspiracy* is that the massive head wound was in back of the skull. Since neither Dr. McClelland or any Parkland staffer turned President Kennedy over onto his stomach, such a wound wouldn't have been visible to them in the first place.

The true professionalism which Groden and Model bring to their topic shows through when one examines the drawings that accompany some of the enhanced Zapruder film frames. In frame 413, for example, about five seconds after the fatal head shot, Groden claims to have spotted an assassin, rifle in hand, through the trees and to the right of the concrete retaining wall. Since the film is not clear enough to warrant an independent determination, Groden obviously felt compelled to help the reader along. The drawing that accompanies the film frame is so amateurish that it could scarcely be credited to a five-year old. Indeed, it has a quality about it that resembles something that came off the drawing boards at Looney Toons.[136]

The same can be said for the drawing that accompanies an extreme blow-up of footage shot by spectator Orville Nix. For years, critics have claimed to discern a man, apparently elevated into mid-air beside a white station wagon, aiming a rifle at the motorcade. The assassin is visible to the west of the concrete pergola on the grassy knoll, where he could have been observed by the dozens of witnesses standing in front of the Depository.

The "assassin" drawn to accompany the Nix photo has, perhaps as a touch of whimsy, been given a jacket and is minus a right eyebrow. To Groden and Model, that's evidence.[137]

Three years later, the House Select Committee would turn its attention to both the Zapruder film segment and the Nix film. The HSCA photographic panel determined that Groden's assassin was actually a bystander on the steps leading up to the grassy knoll, and that the rifle he was holding was a twig and a break in the foliage along the concrete retaining wall. The Nix film's gunman was seen to be chance shadows on the white concrete pergola.[138]

Despite the fact that he was a member of the HSCA photographic panel, Groden displays his mistrust in official conclusions by including the same photos in his new book, *High Treason*.[139] This time, however, the assassin in the Zapruder film is holding what could "possibly" be a rifle,[140] and the gunman in the Nix film now appears at the end of the concrete retaining wall where he had been spotted by David Lifton years before.[141] Indeed, Groden claims to discern a "flash of light" from this apparition behind the wall just at the moment of the fatal head shot,[142] proof yet again that the greatest talent Groden possesses is a creative imagination.

The only thing that *Case for Conspiracy* succeeds in proving is that Groden and Model didn't have much of a case. *High Treason*, on the other hand, is a frightening book. I use the word "frightening" because it's difficult for me to conceive that a normal, rational human being could, in his own mind, develop and then write the distortions, fantasies, and speculations that, in my opinion, *High Treason* contains.

Like *Case for Conspiracy*, *High Treason* is a joint effort between Groden and Harrison Livingstone. Reading the text, though, it's hard to tell who wrote what. Vague references to "the author" don't help much. The reader is left to guess which one is responsible for the statement.

High Treason carries a subtitle, *What Really Happened*. This book is so far removed from reality that it cannot pretend to represent what really happened that day in Dallas. Among the assertions of Groden and Livingstone:

1. *That the autopsy photos and x-rays were altered to conceal a wound at the rear of the head;*[143]

2. *That Lee Oswald was a government contract agent who was targeted in advance to take the blame for the assassination;*[144]

3. *That the CIA is responsible for a massive cover-up after the assassination;*[145]

4. *That the Secret Service was a conspirator in the assassination.*[146]

The House Select Committee, prior to engaging in an effort to determine the trajectory of the bullets that struck the President, authenticated the autopsy photos and x-rays as being those of the late President. Groden asserts that there was, indeed, the massive wound in the rear of Kennedy's head that he, Lifton, and Thompson all conjecture. He further believes that prior to their examination by the HSCA, the autopsy x-rays and photographs were altered so as to fail to depict this wound. He makes much of a technique called "matte edge insertion" which he says could have accomplished this task.

With respect to the x-rays, which clearly show the wound at the side of the head, Groden draws a blank. Instead, he uses a new-found ability to read x-rays and solemnly informs his readers that the x-rays show the right side of Kennedy's face substantially disfigured.[147] Since the autopsy photos show Kennedy's right eye and cheek intact, the x-rays must have been altered as well.

Clearly, Groden cannot read x-rays. The views he publishes in *High Treason* and purport to illustrate the disruption of the President's face are not as representative of structure as a still photograph might be. X-rays penetrate (and thus, reveal) through-and-through the structure.[148] Dr. John Lattimer, who undoubtedly can read x-rays, has examined at length the x-rays and autopsy photos at the National Archives. He wrote me that "the line of breakage is well above the eye socket and face."[149]

It has doubtless not occurred to Groden that Dr. Cyril Wecht, a critic of the Warren Commission who has published several articles regarding his review of the autopsy materials, might have noticed the facial disruption and been eager to report on it. I have copies of Wecht's writings and he does not mention any sort of disfigurement.

The assertion that someone masked out a wound at the rear of the President's head is equally ludicrous. Obviously, such a rear head wound is absent on the x-rays, excepting the small wound of entrance at the top of the skull. The three autopsy doctors ought, by rights, to remember if there was such a wound. When shown the x-rays and photos by the HSCA panel, they did not mention its absence.

Groden has enhanced frames of the Zapruder film taken after the head shot and carefully points out what he believes is the bloody edge of the wound at the back of President Kennedy's head.[150] All I can see is the right edge of Mrs. Kennedy's pink hat.

To buttress his conclusion that someone doctored the autopsy photos and x-rays, Groden cites interviews with the Parkland doctors conducted by co-author Harrison Livingstone. These interviews, which are somewhat contrary in their content to the HSCA findings, prove nothing but the futility of trying to question someone about a twenty-minute time span some fifteen years or more after the fact. Groden and Livingstone, for that matter, don't include the drawings and other material they say they showed to the doctors in order to elicit their "favorable" response. For that reason, it's tough to tell what some of the physicians are talking about.[151]

Much of *High Treason* is aimed at disproving the single-bullet theory. Groden and Livingstone never get around to explaining where the bullet that hit Kennedy might have gone if it didn't hit Connally. Indeed, the authors avoid the question of where the bullets went. Their avoidance is an important consideration since they believe that there may have been as many as seven shots fired, including one from a manhole cover atop the Commerce Street knoll, and another from the triple underpass.[152]

Groden asserts that the Secret Service were conspirators in a plot to assassinate Kennedy because several agents were out late the night before the murder, visiting at a Fort Worth nightclub.[153] He cites as further "proof" the fact that agents were slow to react when the shots were fired.[154] What Groden doesn't mention is that the Secret Service had never been in this kind of situation before, that the echo chamber of Dealey Plaza made identifying gunfire as gunfire a time-consuming task, and that the Warren Commission investigated the agents' behavior the night before and concluded that no agent had violated regulations.[155]

Groden, in his chapter on the assassin, states flatly that Oswald "was trained as an agent."[156] He charges that Oswald's "Historic Diary," pronounced authentic by the HSCA and the Warren Commission, "is clearly fake."[157] *High Treason* offers no evidence to back these assertions, only speculation.

High Treason would be almost comic if it were not so shrill in tone. Apparently, Groden and Livingstone believe that literally everyone involved with the President's trip to Texas is a suspect in his murder,

To many Americans, John and Jacqueline Kennedy were a magical couple. Since his death, the President's image has literally become larger-than-life, leading many to believe that such a powerful and imposing historical figure could only have been killed by a massive, hidden conspiracy. The facts, however, strongly support the opposite conclusion . . . that Kennedy was the victim of a lone assassin who simply made the most of an unfortunate opportunity.
UNITED PRESS INTERNATIONAL/BETTMAN ARCHIVES

The President and Mrs. Kennedy arrived at Dallas' Love Field at 11:37 a.m. on November 22. The Presidential motorcade wound toward downtown, then headed west along Main Street toward Dealey Plaza. DALLAS TIMES HERALD

The crowds along Main Street were so thick that some motorcycle officers could not ride their assigned positions in the motorcade. One patrolman said that the crowds would grab the handlebars and almost pull the cycles over. DALLAS TIMES HERALD

Willis slide 5, perhaps the single most important assassination photo. Willis squeezed the camera shutter as a reflex to the sound of the first shot. In the Zapruder film, one can see Willis has taken his camera down from his eye by frame 204—so this photo must have been snapped at about frame 190. PHIL WILLIS

A New Look at the Zapruder Film

Z-188: At the moment of the first shot, the President is waving to the crowd along Elm Street.

Z-228: For a moment, a road sign obscured the President from Zapruder's view. Most researchers believe Kennedy is reacting to his first wound here. Instead, the President is responding in fright to a first, missed shot.

Z-230: The President's hands are rising to cover his face and Governor Connally is reacting to the sound of the shot.

Z-235: Oswald fires his second shot, which hits the President in the back . . .

Z-237: . . . and goes on to wound Governor Connally.

Z-238: The strike on the Governor is apparent here.

Z-255: The limousine continues to coast down Elm Street, and Jackie finally realizes what has happened to her husband.

Z-312: Oswald's final shot impacts on the back of the President's head, pushing him forward before . . .

Z-313: . . . the bullet exits Kennedy's right temple. An explosion of blood and tissue throws him violently backward.

Z-316: The backward and sideways motion of the President's head and body is apparent here.

Z-322: The President's rearward motion finally ends when his shoulders hit the car seat.

Z-413: The 'assassin' critics saw in this frame what was proven to be twigs and a bystander's head by the House Select Committee.

Riding in the White House Press Pool, photographer Tom Dillard raised his camera and took two shots of the front of the Book Depository seconds after others had spotted a rifle there.
TOM DILLARD, NATIONAL ARCHIVES

Some minutes after the assassination, officers finally begin to seal off the crime scene—but the assassin fled on foot three minutes after the shots were fired. DALLAS TIMES HERALD

Stunned citizens gathered at Parkland Hospital to watch . . . wait . . . and hope.
DALLAS MORNING NEWS

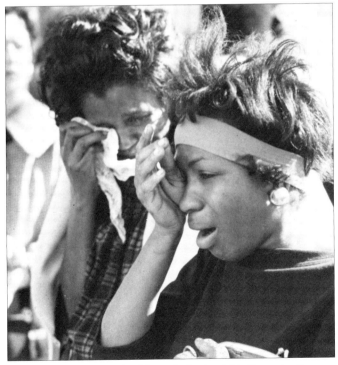

News of the President's death brought fresh grief to those standing
outside the emergency entrance. DALLAS TIMES HERALD

The Italian army rifle had been placed beneath an overhanging row of book boxes, indicating the site of concealment had been carefully planned in advance. NATIONAL ARCHIVES

Dallas police detective J.C. Day holds the rifle out of reach of reporters crowded into police headquarters. NATONAL ARCHIVES

Newsmen and police officers disturbed the arrangement of book boxes in the sniper's perch. This photo was one source for our reconstruction of the corner window area.
NATIONAL ARCHIVES

Oswald was questioned by the Dallas police, the FBI, and the press in an almost madhouse atmosphere at police headquarters. DALLAS TIMES HERALD

"Ready for anything," Lee Harvey Oswald poses in April, 1963, with the weapons used to kill the president and Officer Tippit. Despite the claims of critics, the three Oswald-with-weapons photos are apparently authentic.
NATIONAL ARCHIVES

Further tying Oswald to the rifle which killed the President is this handwritten order form. Oswald paid $21.45 for the rifle which would later kill John F. Kennedy.
NATIONAL ARCHIVES

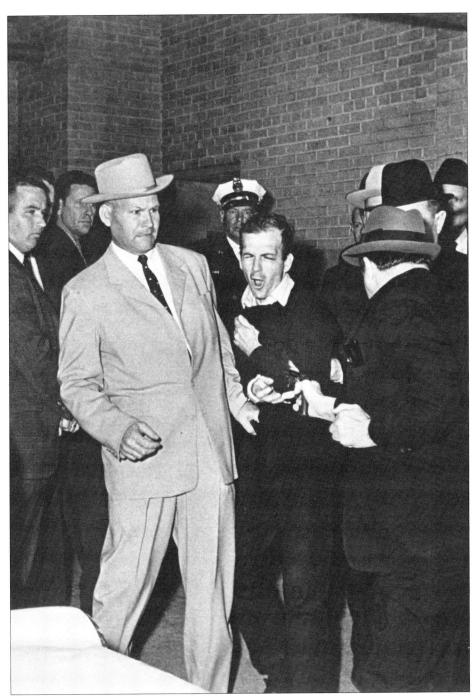

Jack Ruby exacts a nation's revenge on the assassin.   BOB JACKSON

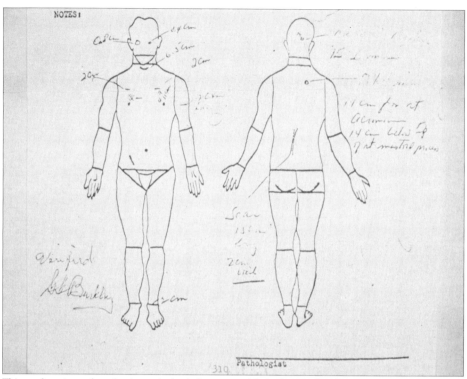

NOTES:

Pathologist

This crude autopsy face sheet was the basis for many critics's charges that the President was hit from the front as well as from above and behind. This diagram was never intended to accurately represent the wound locations, but was used as a worksheet during the autopsy. NATIONAL ARCHIVES

The President's shirt bore mute testimony that he was first struck in the back, not in the neck as the Warren Commission claimed.

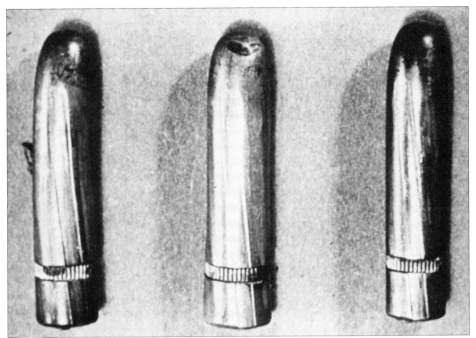

Critics allege that the so-called 'pristine bullet' wasn't deformed enough to have caused Kennedy's neck wound and all of Connally's injuries. CE 399 is in the middle, flanked by two test bullets fired into cotton. Note that the photo is carefully staged so that viewers could not see the flattened side of bullet 399.

The Warren Commission postulated this bullet trajectory through Kennedy's neck—without seeing the autopsy x-rays and photos. The President was leaning forward when he was struck by the second shot, and the actual wound of entry was lower.

The Texas School Book
Depository Building Today

Minus the decorative masonry, the storage shed alongside, and the Hertz Rent-A-Car sign on the roof, the Texas School Book Depository (now the Dallas County Administration Building) appears much as it did in 1963. TRUITT PHOTOGRAPHICS

Visitors trek through the Sixth Floor exhibit for a look at the window Oswald used. At left, the Moorman photograph can be seen at the end of the walkway. Many critics have used this much-damaged Polaroid to shore up their theories of gunmen atop the grassy knoll. TRUITT PHOTOGRAPHICS

Author Jim Moore in the sniper's perch. Reconstructing the corner window was the high point of his 23-year obsession with the Kennedy assassination. Compare the arrangement of boxes to the photo below, taken immediately after the assassination in 1963.

Why stall around in high school?

By BILL HUSTED
Democrat Staff Writer

KNOXVILLE — James Moore is 17 years old, a child of the times.

What a time. What a child.

Moore plans to be president of the United States someday. Moore's timetable is so definite that he must skip his senior year in high school and graduate from college in an election year.

Before he takes that on, he wants to find out who killed President John F. Kennedy. He intends to prove that Lee Harvey Oswald didn't do it by himself. To that end, Moore has traveled to Dallas three times to interview eyewitnesses to the killing.

What kind of nut is this?

"I guess you could say I'm a conspiracy nut," Moore said. "When I hear about something, I start thinking that there must be a conspiracy."

Moore, an A and B student at nearly Lamar High School in Johnson County, is no kind of nut. He, like all of us, is a product of the times.

The year he was born, a man named Fidel Castro was seizing power in Cuba. When Moore was 4, Kennedy was killed. Neil Armstrong was setting foot on the moon the year Moore turned 10. President Richard Nixon became the first president to resign in Moore's 15th year.

Arkansas Album

And Moore has tried to follow the woofs and warps of his world.

It has been a world of obsessions.

Moore spent three years of his life trying to learn everything he could about Baron Manfred von Richthofen, the World War I German flying ace. He took a year or so on Harry Houdini, the escape artist and magician.

"I've always been interested in odd things," Moore said.

But his interest in the Kennedy assassination is no passing fancy. Moore has chewed and digested books and pamphlets detailing the various theories of conspiracy. He has studied ballistics reports, examined handwriting samples and talked to witnesses with a grim sense of purpose—unusually grim, amazingly serious, for a 17-year-old.

"It's important to me because, if we can prove that the government has lied to us, then we can assume there have been other incidents of deceit that have yet to be uncovered," Moore said. "I have become quite cynical of everything the government has done."

Cynicism comes easily, even naturally, for Moore.

"I am cynical of the men that run government, disbelieving of their actions," he said.

And does he wonder sometimes if his life is too serious, not enough play and too many plots?

"I like to think I am serious," he said. "I can't see that I'm missing too much in being serious. Maybe someday I'll look back and be sorry, but I don't think so."

Moore's conspiracy theories—whether they are given any credence or not—are frightening to grow up with.

"My father told me that one of these guys (the visitors that come to interview Moore) will knock on the door with a shotgun someday," Moore said.

But, at least for a moment, Moore smiled.

"I don't believe anyone is going to drive this far to shoot me," he said.

He lives in an isolated spot at the end of a road that stops at his front door.

His interest in politics seems a hopeful sign in a young man who believes government cannot be believed. It is the people who are in office that he distrusts, not the system.

Moore sounded like a politican when he talked of his plans.

"I want to go as high as I can go," he said, and then immediately seemed to regret his words. "People think you are

an egotist if you say you want to be president.

"I want to start in local politics and gradually work up."

So he is trying to enter Arkansas Polytechnic College at Russellville this fall.

"I can't see any use of waiting around for my senior year in high school," he said. "I want to get started."

An interview with seventeen-year-old Moore in the *Arkansas Democrat*, July 26, 1976, details the early development of his "obsession."

that Oswald is totally innocent and the investigative bodies which have reviewed the crime have all been dedicated to maintaining some sort of cover-up. Asserting that Oswald was trained by the United States government and then sent to Russia as a "defector" is one thing, but asserting that the training extended some years later to the assassination of an American President is quite another.

It's worth noting that, while serving on the HSCA photographic evidence panel, Groden was a lone dissenter. In *High Treason*, he claims that he was coached on what to say during public hearings and then denied the chance to expound his views in closed session. Strangely enough, the Committee did publish his allegation that the autopsy photos had been forged, and his testimony doesn't read as you might expect it to read if Groden had been coached.

With this thought in mind, the time has come to ask a crucial question: Are the abilities of men and women like Groden superior to those of everyone else? Were people like Thomas Buchanan, Mark Lane, Jay Epstein, Sylvia Meagher and Harold Weisberg just smarter than the Warren Commission members and staff? Are people like Robert Groden and David Lifton better at investigating the events of November 22, 1963, than members of the House Select Committee on Assassinations?

And what is it that people like Groden, Lifton, and Weisberg see in photographs that eludes the rest of us? How can a single frame of film reveal an assassin to someone like Groden, and leaves and twigs to the House Select Committee? How can Groden detect forgery in an autopsy photograph, and yet the doctors who performed the autopsy notice nothing wrong?

And how is it that the critics demand accountability from the investigations they first incite and then deplore, but provide no accountability of their own? Where are the other four bullets Groden claims were fired in Dealey Plaza? Where did they go? Why, after more than twenty-six years of diligent research, have the critics not been able to name a single name, find a single bullet not fired from Oswald's rifle, locate someone who actually saw another gunman firing at the President, or provide concrete evidence of crossfire and conspiracy?

The American public has a fascination with conspiracy. The crime that robbed us of President Kennedy seems too massive to be attributed to a single, demented man. But truth is often stranger, and certainly more valuable than fiction. And until the critics produce some answers of their own, we have every right to regard their speculation and innuendo as the less valuable of the two.

Just as this chapter does not end this book, so it will not end the often irresponsible speculation of the critics. Nor should it. We live in a free society, and the views of the dissenters should be encouraged. What should not be tolerated is the all-too-evident ability of the critics to create their own fortunes from the ignorance and remorse of the American public.

---

1. Miller, 218.
2. Roberts, 117.
3. Ibid.
4. Ibid., 118.
5. Ibid.
6. Ibid., 119.
7. Lane, 340.
8. Letter to the author, December 1989.
9. Anson, 73.
10. Miller, 74.
11. Ibid.
12. Anson, 74.
13. Ibid., 71.
14. Ibid.
15. Ibid.
16. Ibid., 72.
17. Roberts, 121.
18. Ibid.
19. Ibid.
20. Ibid.
21. Ibid.
22. Ibid.
23. Ibid.
24. Ibid.
25. Ibid.
26. Lane, 96.
27. Roberts, 120.
28. Ibid.
29. Ibid.
30. Ibid.
31. Miller, 3.
32. Belin, 470.
33. Ibid.
34. Ibid., 472.
35. Ibid.
36. Ibid.
37. Ibid.
38. Ibid
39. Ibid.
40. Ibid.
41. Ibid., 473.
42. Miller, 179.
43. Undated letter to the author.
44. Ibid.
45. Letter to the author, March 18, 1975.
46. Roberts, 122.
47. Ibid.
48. Ibid.
49. Ibid.
50. Ibid.
51. *Newsweek*, November 14, 1966, 30.
52. Ibid.
53. Ibid.
54. Ibid.
55. Ibid.

56. Ibid.
57. Ibid.
58. Ibid.
59. Epstein, *Legend: the Secret World of Lee Harvey Oswald*, (New York: McGraw-Hill, 1978).
60. Ibid., 242.
61. Ibid., 368.
62. Penn Jones, Jr., *Forgive My Grief*, (Midlothian, Texas: The Midlothian Mirror, 1966), 184.
63. Ibid., 185.
64. Roberts, 96.
65. Ibid.
66. Jones, 98.
67. Ibid., 22.
68. Roberts, 97.
69. Jones, 65.
70. Miller, 40.
71. Ibid., 15.
72. Ibid., 14.
73. Letter to the author, March 18, 1975.
74. Weisberg, 33.
75. Ibid., 205.
76. Weisberg, *Whitewash II: the FBI-Secret Service Cover-up*, (Hyattstown, Maryland, self-published, 1966), 218.
77. Letter to the author, April 22, 1975.
78. Groden and Livingstone, 187.
79. Letter to the author, March 18, 1975.
80. Weisberg, 184.
81. John Sparrow, *After the Assassination*, (New York: Chilmark Press, 1967), 73.
82. Ibid.
83. Thompson, 193.
84. Thompson, 223.
85. Sixth Floor Exhibit Audio Tour, Antenna Productions, 1989.
86. Richard H. Popkin,*The Second Oswald*, (New York: New York Review,1966), 92.
87. Ibid., 1.
83. Ibid., 103.
89. Ibid., 105.
90. Sparrow, 47.
91. Popkin. 81.
92. Ibid., 62.
93. Ibid., 97.
94. Anson, 70.
95. Miller, 171.
96. David S. Lifton, *Best Evidence*, (New York: Dell Publishing, 1980), 18.
97. Ibid.,17.
98. Ibid., 18.
99. Ibid., 65.
100. Ibid.
101. Ibid., 59.
102. Ibid., 31.
103. Ibid., 30.
104. Groden and Livingstone, 35.
105. Lifton, 383.
106. *USA Today* television program, February 20, 1989.
107. Lifton, 245.
108. Telephone conversation with Dr. Lattimer, November 15, 1989.
109. Ibid.
110. Ibid.

111. Ibid.
112. Lattimer, 153.
113. Lifton, 54.
114. Lifton, 66.
115. Ibid., 474.
116. Ibid., 868.
117. Ibid.
118. Ibid.
119. Ibid., 870.
120. Miller, 179.
121. Ibid., 44.
122. Groden and model, 129.
123. Groden and Livingstone, 412.
124. Robert Cutler, *Z-313*, (Manchester, Massachusetts: Cutler Designs, February 11, 1975).
125. Groden and Model, 25.
126. Ibid., 149.
127. HSCA, VI, 310.
128. Groden and Model, 35.
129. Ibid., 35-39.
130. Ibid., 72.
131. Ibid., 8.
132. Ibid., 73.
133. Ibid., 75.
134. Ibid., 79.
135. Ibid., 83.
136. Ibid., 134.
137. Ibid., 135.
138. HSCA, VI, 131.
139. Groden and Livingstone. Photo section prior to chapter 13.
140. Ibid.
141. Ibid.
142. Ibid.
143. Ibid., 88.
144. Ibid., 143.
145. Ibid., 286-287.
146. Ibid., 137.
147. Ibid., 72, 396.
148. Lattimer, letter to the author, December 1, 1989.
149. Ibid.
150. Groden and Livingstone. Photo opposite 391.
151. Ibid., 37 et al.
152. Ibid. First photo section, third page.
153. Ibid., 129.
154. Ibid., 127.
155. WCR, 426.
156. Groden and Livingstone, 140.
157. Ibid., 143.

CHAPTER

VII

Pictures Don't Lie

MUCH OF THE CONTROVERSY SURROUNDING THE ASSASSINATION of President Kennedy has been generated by what researchers and the public think they see in photographs. I've already mentioned that grassy knoll assassins have been proven to be twigs and shadows, but a deeper exploration of the photographic evidence is in order.

There were more than twenty photographers present in Dealey Plaza that Friday afternoon; almost all were amateurs. The still and motion pictures they exposed give us an almost panoramic view of the assassination. During the past fifteen years, one photographer's work has stood above and beyond all the rest in conveying the horror of the President's murder. The cameraman's name was Abraham Zapruder. Zapruder was a Dallas dress manufacturer. His firm, Jennifer Juniors, was located in the Dal-Tex building just across Houston Street from the Depository. Although he had just acquired a new Bell & Howell movie camera, Zapruder left it at home that Friday morning because the skies were dark and threatening. His secretary, Lillian Rogers, persuaded him to return to his residence and retrieve the camera.[1] Then, the couple set out to find a good vantage point from which to film the motorcade. Other office workers joined them.[2]

They chose a concrete pedestal atop the grassy knoll, just beyond a part of the retaining wall that runs from the pergola to the flight of steps leading down the hill. The pedestal raised Zapruder some four feet above the gently sloping hillside. To his left, two hundred feet away, was the Texas School Book Depository building. Elm Street curved directly in front of him and the President of the United States would pass within yards of his camera lens.

Looking through the viewfinder, Zapruder, who suffered from vertigo, began to lose his balance. He asked his receptionist, Marilyn Sitzman, to stand behind him on the pedestal and steady him as he photographed the motorcade. Photos taken of the scene show Zapruder leaning into his viewfinder and Sitzman looking down onto Elm Street over Zapruder's left shoulder.

From their vantage point, Zapruder and Sitzman saw the lead car of the motorcade swing into the intersection at Main and Houston. It was followed by the Presidential limousine. As the long, midnight blue Lincoln turned onto Elm making a hairpin turn directly in front of the Book Depository, Zapruder pressed the shutter release. The result was the most carefully scrutinized twenty-two seconds of motion picture film ever recorded.

What Zapruder, Sitzman and the other eyewitnesses saw as the motorcade wound down Elm Street can best be described in a frame-by-frame analysis of the film itself. I have lived with the Zapruder film for more than fifteen years. I have watched my own Robert Groden-enhanced version literally hundreds of times and have had individual slides made so that I could more closely study crucial frames. Only Groden and Josiah Thompson, who served as *Life's* consultant and had unlimited access to the original film have spent more time with Zapruder's movie than I have.

The motion picture actually serves as a clock of the assassination. We know Zapruder's camera—it ran at 18.3 frames per second. Therefore, we can determine in a frame-for-frame analysis how much time is passing between events. As we'll see, this information is critical to the determination of how the President was killed.

The Zapruder film frames are numbered from the onset of the film through the assassination and until Zapruder stopped filming. Beginning around frame 190, something odd appears in the film's background. Rosemary Willis, the daughter of retired Air Force Major Phil Willis, has been running down the Elm Street curve in preceding frames. Now, she suddenly stops and looks back up Elm, toward the Depository.[3] The HSCA identifies Rosemary only as "a young girl."[4]

A half-second later, at approximately frame 200, the President's movements suddenly freeze. Kennedy's hand stops in mid-wave, and his head begins a turn from his right toward the left in the direction of Mrs. Kennedy.[5] Barely a third of a second later, at Zapruder frame 207, the President disappears behind a road sign that blocked Zapruder's view of the limousine for about a second.

But that second is crucial. When Kennedy reappears at Zapruder frame 225, something is obviously wrong. The President's hands move rapidly toward his face, leading most observers to believe that he has just been struck by a bullet.[6]

Governor Connally also appears to be reacting to some extraordinary event. As he reappears from behind the road sign, he is frowning, and there is a clear stiffening of his shoulders and upper body.[7] In succeeding frames, the facial expression changes again, and there is considerable movement of the Governor's head.[8]

Indeed, within the next quarter-second, we see Governor Connally suddenly raise his white Stetson hat—he's holding it in his right hand—to chest height.[9] He also begins to turn to his left. Then in 1/18 of a second, between frames 237 and 238, Connally's right shoulder is driven downward, his cheeks puff, and his hair is mussed.[10] Josiah Thompson notes that the Governor, in frame 238, "gives the appearance of someone who has just had the wind knocked out of him."[11]

The President's hands, still in front of his face, rapidly descend to clutch at his throat. By frame 255, Kennedy is bent forward, straining against his back brace, and his hands are clenched at his chin.

The Presidential limousine continues to coast downhill. One notices green grass in the background, and motionless spectators as well. Jean Hill and Mary Moorman slide by, as does Charles Brehm with his young son. Governor Connally is falling into his wife's arms, and Mrs. Kennedy is leaning toward her husband, wondering desperately what is wrong.

Suddenly, at frame 312, the President's head moves forward, in an almost unseen blur. At frame 313, there is an explosion of blood and brain tissue from the right side of Kennedy's skull, and a piece of bone can be seen rocketing several feet into the air.[12] The dying President, with his wife looking on in horror, is slammed backward and to his left immediately following the bullet's impact. The backward motion finally stops when Kennedy's body hits the car seat cushion.

The hole in the right side of his head clearly visible, Kennedy begins to fall to the left, into his wife's lap. Mrs. Kennedy begins scrambling up, almost fighting her way out of the back seat and onto the trunk of the Presidential limousine. She is probably reaching for a fragment of the President's skull that was driven up and over the car deck.

As Mrs. Kennedy, her elbow on the top of the cushion, begins to crawl out of the back seat, we see AP newsman James Altgens, with camera in hand, frozen in shock on the south side of Elm Street. By the time her knees reach the cushion top, Secret Service Agent Clint Hill has raced to the car, has a foot on the bumper, and is reaching for the handholds at the rear of the trunk.

Hill leaves his feet, climbs onto the bumper, and stretches to push Mrs. Kennedy back down into the car seat where the President lies motionless. The Zapruder film ends as the auto races into the darkness of the triple underpass. The eastern side of the wooden fence atop the grassy knoll is captured in the last few frames of the film.

Zapruder kept the film running through his camera, even though he heard the shots and saw the Governor stricken and the President mortally wounded. As the limousine raced under the overpass, Zapruder was screaming, "They killed him."[13] Seconds after the shooting, Zapruder and Sitzman had climbed down from their pedestal and stumbled toward office workers seeking safety in the shadows of the concrete pergola.[14] For Zapruder, the terror had really only begun. Chosen by destiny to record the assassination for history, he would be forever haunted by the specter of what he had seen through his camera viewfinder. Within days *Life* magazine would pay him an initial $25,000 for his film. But the money only meant additional security for his family. The enormity of what he had seen and filmed would dog him for the rest of his days.

Diagonally across Dealey Plaza from Zapruder and Sitzman, Orville Nix and Marie Muchmore were filming the motorcade with their own motion picture cameras. Indeed, Nix ran across the Plaza to catch the Presidential party before the limousine ran beneath the triple underpass.

Both the Muchmore and Nix films were purchased by UPI and

selected frames from each were subsequently published in *Four Days*, a large, well-written primer on the assassination that appeared on newsstands shortly after the turn of the year.[15]

The Muchmore film is the closer, brighter, and more detailed of the two. The Presidential Lincoln coasts down Elm Street, and William and Gayle Newman are visible on the curb just beyond the President. Charles Brehm and his son, along with Beverly Oliver, come into view and trail to the right as the camera pans leftward. Jean Hill, wearing her red raincoat, stares intently at the President with Mary Moorman standing beside her, ready to take her final Polaroid photo.

At the top of the frame, the bottom of the wooden fence atop the grassy knoll is also visible. On the stairs, three spectators watch the Presidential limousine pass in front of them. A moment before, there had been only two men on the steps leading down from the knoll. Emmet Hudson, the groundskeeper of Dealey Plaza, joined the pair just as the Lincoln began descending the Elm Street slope.*

The moment of the fatal head shot is somewhat obscured in the Muchmore film; Moorman and Hill, along with a motorcycle officer's helmet, block our view. But the backwards head-snap is clearly evident in the Nix film in both black-and-white and in color. Both are equally disturbing. The last few frames of the Nix film show the Presidential limousine speeding away under the triple overpass, and the trio of men on the stairway beginning to run, panic-stricken.[16]

Standing at the corner of Main and Houston Streets, spectator Robert Hughes shot his own color movie as the President passed by. His film is the only one in which it is possible to view all at one time the Presidential limousine, the Book Depository building, and the sixth-floor window. Hughes stopped filming just as the Lincoln turned the corner from Houston onto Elm Street.

Apparently, the FBI studied one frame of his film and could discern no visible human form in the sixth-floor window. Years after the Warren Commission Report, in which Hughes' film was not even mentioned, a House Select Committee analysis determined that the film showed no visible movement in the window.[17]

---

* *Hudson can be seen, head and shoulders, behind the concrete retaining wall in Phil Willis' fifth slide. Critics have interpreted the "blob" in Willis' photo as an assassin.*[18]

Another film, from nearly the same vantage point, was shot by spectator Charles L. Bronson minutes before the assassination.[19] The HSCA didn't have an opportunity to review the Bronson film with as much care and detail as they had given the Hughes strip.[20] So, while the panel believed that no movement appeared in the sixth-floor window, it did note that the high quality of the motion picture warranted further study.[21]

Most casual readers of assassination literature are unaware that a film was actually taken from a Book Depository window as the Presidential limousine made its way down Houston Street and negotiated the turn onto Elm. Shot by Elsie Dorman, the film ends seconds short of the first shot.[22] Mrs. Dorman filmed from the Depository's fourth floor, and is visible in the Hughes film, taken a block south on Houston Street.

John Martin was standing at the corner of Houston and Elm, motion picture camera in hand. The HSCA published a frame from his footage of the assassination's aftermath because it showed, in profile, Billy Nolan Lovelady, the Depository employee who was standing in the building's doorway as the shots were fired. Seen in the Altgens photo from further down the south side of Elm Street, Lovelady was originally believed by many critics to have been Lee Harvey Oswald. The HSCA used Martin's film to show that the shirt Lovelady was wearing after the assassination was identical to the one worn by the man in the doorway.[23]

More than a dozen photographers shot still pictures of the motorcade at or near the time of the assassination. The Warren Commission published some of the most visible and ignored many others. For example, the Commission didn't acknowledge the existence of the series taken by spectator Wilma Bond. Already mentioned in this book, the Bond slides are interesting not because they show the assassination, but because they show its aftermath. Eyewitnesses and motorcycle officers are clearly visible racing up the grassy knoll after the departure of the Presidential limousine.*

---

*The still Polaroid taken by Mary Moorman was not published by the Commission. Indeed, it was overlooked by many early critics as well. Researcher David Lifton "discovered" the Moorman photo for himself in a memorial book on the assassination.[24]

Retired Air Force Major Phil Willis took a series of sixteen color slides immediately before, during, and after the assassination. Willis was standing near the curb at the corner of Houston and Elm Streets when he took his fifth slide, certainly the most controversial of the dozen-odd photos he snapped that day.[25]

Slide five was taken a fraction of a second after the first shot was fired. Willis told the Warren Commission about slide five ". . . my next shot was taken at the very—in fact, the shot caused me to squeeze the camera shutter, and I got a picture of the President as he was hit with the first shot. So instantaneous, in fact, that the crowd hadn't had time to react."[26]

Although I regard Willis' fifth slide as one of the most critical assassination photos, I disagree with his assertion that his picture portrays "the President as he was hit with the first shot." I do not doubt, however, that Willis took the slide immediately after the first shot was fired.

Indeed, Willis is visible in the Zapruder film until frame 206, the frame prior to the one in which President Kennedy is last visible before he goes behind the Stemmons Freeway sign. Harold Weisberg noted in a letter to me that, "Actually, in the Zapruder film, one can see that Willis has taken his camera down from his eye before frame 205."[27]

The House Select Committee determined that Willis had taken slide five at about frame 202 of the Zapruder film. As you'll note in the next chapter, the HSCA reconstruction of the assassination shot sequence contradicted Willis' testimony. And, unfortunately for the HSCA, Willis is one of the few assassination witnesses who possesses a keen and accurate memory of the event.*

Why the concern about the instant at which Willis took his fifth slide? Because the Warren Commission re-enactment determined that Oswald's view of the motorcade was blocked by leaves of a large oak tree until frame 210. Except for a brief instant at frame 186, when the President appeared between branches, Oswald did not have a clear line of fire until after Willis took his slide. And Willis maintains that the first shot caused him to take the photo.

---

* *Willis was also at Pearl Harbor on December 7, 1941.*

Willis' fifth slide forms an important link in the chain of evidence that will help us determine how the President was killed. As we'll see in a later chapter, I believe that the photo was taken earlier than either the Warren Commission or the HSCA believed. Willis' eighth slide has been subjected to critical analysis as well. The slide, captioned "The Search for the Assassin Already Begun," shows the front of the Depository some minutes after the assassination. The slide is of interest because it appears to show Jack Ruby at the assassination site. Dressed in a white shirt and dark suit, the man resembling Ruby can be found at the right edge of the photograph. Walking past a policeman, the man appears about to step off the sidewalk in front of the Depository into Houston Street.

Willis told me in a telephone conversation that the mounting process sometimes obscured "Ruby" from the slide view. In other words, if the slide were viewed in a holder or printed that way, a substantial portion of the man's face would not be visible.[28] "Take the slide out of the mount," Willis patiently told me, "and he's in there big as life."[29]

In *Rush to Judgment*, Mark Lane decried the version of slide eight published by the Warren Commission as further evidence of the cover-up. In discussing the Willis slides, Lane notes: "The Commission did publish all twelve photographs, but it offered an incomplete print of slide eight. Its version differs from the original . . . As published by the Commission, the picture was trimmed in such a manner that a substantial portion of the face of the man thought to be Ruby was removed.[30]

Here is another example of the extent of Lane's respect for basic investigation and research. The Commission simply printed the slides as they appeared within their holders. The Citizens' Commission of Inquiry investigator who called on Willis in 1964 was not interested in the photographic process so much as raising another bit of doubt in the mind of the American public.*

The Willis "original" seen by the CCI representative is a large, eight-by-eleven-inch color print made from the unmounted slide.[31]

---

* *The issue at question is whether Ruby was telling the truth when he claimed to be at the* Dallas Morning News *during the noon hour. Eyewitnesses placed Ruby in Dealey Plaza (where the Willis slide indicates he may have been) and at Parkland Hospital as well.*

Lane, however, does not mention this fact. When confronted with the question, I did something Mark Lane didn't bother to do: I went to Willis' home and looked at the original photographs myself.

In preparing the Sixth Floor exhibit we enlarged the Moorman photograph to nearly wall size for use as a centerpiece leading to the corner window display. The Moorman photo, already referred to in this book, is a black-and-white Polaroid taken by eyewitness Mary Moorman. She was standing next to her friend Jean Hill along the south curb of Elm Street when the shots were fired.

The Moorman photograph roughly corresponds to the head-shot sequence in the Zapruder film, somewhere around frames 313 to 315. It is the only close-range photograph in which one can view both the President and the wooden fence atop the grassy knoll.

The consequences of Moorman's choice to use a Polaroid are staggering. First, she was able to view the photo almost immediately after the shooting, and she, other witnesses, and the press subjected the photo to much mishandling. Second, she was unable to retain any negative. The passing years have not been kind to the Moorman photo. The House Select Committee noted that it had deteriorated over the years, and that, despite new enhancement techniques, it did not yield any new information.[32]

Nonetheless, the Moorman photo is worthy of attention simply because so many critics base theories upon it. In *Six Seconds in Dallas* Josiah Thompson attempted to analyze the photograph in an effort to precisely locate the position of a second assassin behind the wooden fence atop the grassy knoll.[33] The results of Dr. Thompson's conjecture were less than impressive, even to readers with perfect eyesight.

Not content to merely sensationalize a grainy Polaroid copy, Thompson then took his "particularly clear copy"* to Dealey Plaza and showed it to Mark Lane's star witness, Sam Holland. In his book, Thompson records the comments Holland made as he studied the photograph: "Well, now you have something here . . . I didn't see this man before . . . well, do you know, I think you're looking right down the barrel of that gun right now!"[34]

---

* *There is no such thing as a "particularly clear copy" of the Moorman photograph. Underexposed, grainy, and mishandled, even the original is not "particularly clear."*

It doesn't take a perceptive reader to note that Holland apparently saw no man at all until Dr. Thompson helpfully pointed out the alleged second assassin. Thompson then escorted Holland behind the wooden fence, had him stand in the position Thompson claims was occupied by the assassin, then took Holland's photo from street-level. Predictably, Thompson then included the picture as evidence' in his book.[35]

High Treason author Robert Groden thoughtfully provides his readers with an arrow at the spot on the Moorman photograph where he believes the second gunman was located. Later in the book, in a reference to the acoustical tests undertaken by the House Select Committee, Groden almost casually mentions the photo: " . . . the testers placed a shooter at a point on the stockade fence near where witnesses and the Mooreman [sic] photograph had indicated another sniper was located."[36]

The Moorman photograph is not otherwise discussed in *High Treason*. Indeed, since Groden and co-author Harrison Livingstone managed to misspell the name of the photographer, one may well argue that it wasn't mentioned at all.

The House Select Committee took a vastly different view of the Moorman photograph: "Viewing the photograph with the naked eye, one could detect images that might be construed as something significant behind the stockade fence. The images may, however, only represent parts of a tree, or they may be photographic artifacts."[37] The Committee went on to call the significance of the Moorman photo "largely negative."[38] In a word, the critics seem to see what they want to see, evidenced by the way in which writers like Groden and Thompson have treated the Moorman photograph over the years.

THE FINAL PHOTOGRAPHS WE SHOULD DISCUSS do not directly relate to the assassination itself. Rather, they were taken in Dallas some months before and depict Lee Harvey Oswald with the weapons he used to kill President Kennedy and Officer Tippit.

Oswald was shown these photos after his arrest. He claimed that they were forged by placing his head on someone else's body.[39] The critics have a good deal at stake with these photographs. If they are indeed faked, they represent proof of a plot to kill the President and incriminate Oswald. If real, they strongly tie Oswald to the murder weapons. The Warren Commission examined two photos of Oswald with the weapons. They are both essentially the same except for Oswald's stance. In the first, Commission Exhibit 133-A, he holds the rifle in his left hand and two newspapers in his right. The papers are held directly beneath his chin. In the second photo, Commission Exhibit 133-B, Oswald holds the rifle in the right hand and papers in his left. Rather than having his hands close to his body, Oswald is holding both rifle and papers significantly away.[40]

A third Oswald-with-weapons photo was obtained in late 1976 by the House Select Committee from the widow of a Dallas Police Department employee. The committee, following the Warren Commission numbering procedure, designated this photo as 133-C.[41] Finally, in the spring of 1977, HSCA investigators discovered a print of 133-A in the belongings of Oswald's friend, George de Mohrenschildt.[42] Significantly, the photo bore an inscription from Lee Oswald to de Mohrenschildt on the reverse side.[43]*

Marina Oswald told the Warren Commission that, while the Oswalds lived in a rented house on Dallas' Neely Street, they enjoyed a small backyard. One Sunday, while Marina was hanging diapers, Oswald asked her to take photos of him dressed almost entirely in black with the pistol in its holster at his hip, the Mannlicher-Carcano rifle in his hand and copies of leftist newspapers clutched in his fist.[44]

Marina at first remembered taking only one photograph. Later, she recalled taking two. The evidence indicates that she took three.[45] Only one negative was recovered. The HSCA could not elicit an explanation from the Dallas Police as to what had happened to the other two.

Critics have made a variety of charges about the photographs:

1. *A line at Oswald's chin shows that his head was pasted onto someone else's body.*

2. *The shadows that fall from his nose and from his body are inconsistent.*

---

* Subsequently, the Dallas Police Department turned over first generation prints of 133-A and 133-C, thus authenticating (at least insofar as the Dallas Police were concerned) 133-C which the Warren Commission never saw and, apparently never knew existed. [46]

127

3. *The man in the photos appears to have a squarish chin, while Oswald's was cleft.*

4. *The man in the photos changes height from one snapshot to the next.*

5. *The rifle he is holding is longer than the rifle discovered in the Book Depository.*

6. *The photos bear evidence of retouching.*

7. *The background in each photo is the same, while a man-with-weapons photo has been superimposed onto it.*

The HSCA, after exhaustive analysis, determined that all three Oswald-with-weapons photos were authentic. Point-by-point, the Committee's photographic panel refuted the arguments of the critics that the pictures had somehow been faked in an attempt to incriminate Oswald.[47] The Committee, in an effort to beat the critics at their own game, decided to imply some questions of its own:

"Aside from the obvious question of whether Oswald would place his signature on a fake photo, for the photograph to have been faked would have required access, within just a ten-day period, to Oswald's backyard, his camera, rifle (knowing that this would be the assassination weapon), and newspapers. Moreover, a fundamental question is whether a sophisticated conspirator would expose himself to unnecessary risks of detection by making three fake photographs, when just one would suffice."[48]

The Committee further noted that graphite marks on two of the photos indicated that the film had been developed by a drug store or a camera store's photo-finishing service. The photographic panel noted that "it is unlikely that a sophisticated conspirator would have given the end product of his doctoring efforts to a drugstore for printing."[49]

The fact that the photos had been taken in Oswald's camera to the exclusion of all other cameras in the world, and that one copy bore Oswald's authenticated signature would have been enough to convince me that the pictures were, indeed, genuine. But the critics have their entire case at stake and are, therefore, more than usually skeptical.

High Treason author Robert Groden prints poor copies of the three photos and states flatly in the caption that "these pictures were forged in advance of the assassination to make Oswald appear violent, and show him with weapons allegedly used in the murders of President Kennedy and Police Officer J.D. Tippit."[50] Groden notes that the line at

Oswald's chin—suggesting that his head had been photographed atop someone else's body—becomes more pronounced in successive generations of photos.[51] Being a photo analyst, Groden should know that this effect will always be the case when a photo is copied. Since detail is lost with each successive copy, disconnected lines in the original will eventually give the impression of a continuous line.[52] The original photos, which Groden has had the opportunity to work with, do not show any kind of line extending all the way across Oswald's chin. The only thing shown in the region is the cleft beneath his lower lip. In *High Treason*, however, the line becomes quite apparent, and has obviously been added to the photograph.[53]

It's nice to know that when the evidence in this case doesn't fit your own personal point of view, you can always depend on a critic to alter it for you.

Anthony Summers, in his 1980 book, *Conspiracy*, cites the public statements made by Detective Superintendent Malcolm Thompson, a British photographic expert, who had strongly questioned the authenticity of the Oswald-with-weapons photos.[54] The HSCA sent Thompson a draft copy of the photographic analysis of the photographs, and asked for comment.[55] Indeed, Thompson was given an opportunity to testify before the Committee.[56] After studying the report, however, Thompson deferred to the photographic panel's conclusions that the backyard photos bore no evidence of forgery.[57]

Complimentary of the depth of the panel's investigation, and admitting that he had seen only copies of the photos rather than the originals, Thompson still reserved judgment on the apparent shape of Oswald's chin.[58]

Those who expected Summers to include Thompson's change of opinion in his book are, of course, sadly mistaken. Indeed, Summers turned his book into a home video production some time after the HSCA had issued its report. In the video Summers uses an apparently outdated interview with Thompson as proof that the backyard photos were forged. The fact that Thompson had changed his opinion in the interim seems to have made no impression on Summers.[59]

Every serious photo analyst has but one motto: I don't know what I see, I know what I measure. But the critics have managed to con the

American public into deciding that the truth is still at large in the Kennedy assassination. In effect, they've done it by damning scientific analysis of the evidence and instead asserting that the only real measuring stick is what appears evident to the naked eye.*

In sensationalizing the Kennedy assassination photographs, the critics have rendered a grave disservice to the American public. But, as President Kennedy himself noted, history will be the final judge of their deeds. Legend has been created from myth, and public opinion from the stuff dreams are made of.

---

* *Sixth Floor Project Director Conover Hunt credits Robert Groden with almost single-handedly convincing Congress of the need for the House Select Committee investigation. Many Congressmen supported the new probe after viewing Groden's enhanced Zapruder film.* [60]

1. Thompson, op cit,1.
2. Ibid.
3. HSCA, VI, 17.
4. Ibid.
5. Ibid.
6. Ibid.
7. Ibid.
8. Ibid.
9. *Newsweek*, December 5, 1966, 25.
10. Thompson, 93.
11. Ibid., 89.
12. Lattimer, 248.
13. Thompson, 7.
14. Ibid., 3.
15. *Four Days*, United Press International, (American Heritage: New York, 1964).
16. Lifton, ibid., first photo section.
17. United Press International, ibid., 21.
18. HSCA, VI, 119.
19. Ibid., 120.
20. Ibid.
21. Ibid.
22. *Life in Camelot*, Philip B. Kunhardt Jr., Ed., (Little, Brown, and Co.: New York, 1988), 280.
23. HSCA, VI, 288.
24. Lifton, ibid., 28.
25. Weisberg, *Whitewash II*, ibid., 142.
26. 7H, 493.
27. Letter to the author, March 9, 1975.
28. Telephone conversation with the author, August 21, 1978.
29. Ibid.
30. Lane, ibid., 296.
31. Ibid., 223.
32. HSCA, VI, 126.
33. Thompson, ibid., 167.
34. Ibid., 170.
35. Ibid., 168.
36. Groden and Livingstone, ibid., 210.
37. HSCA, *Report*, 84.
38. Ibid., 85.
39. HSCA, VI, 139.
40. Ibid, 145.
41. Ibid, 141.
42. Ibid.
43. HSCA, *Report*, 56.
44. HSCA, *Report*, 56.
45. HSCA, VI, 141.
46. WCR, 120.
47. Ibid., 138-225.
48. HSCA, VI, 177.
49. Ibid.
50. Groden and Livingstone, ibid., third photo section.
51. Ibid.
52. HSCA, VI, 163.
53. Groden and Livingstone, ibid., third photo section.
54. Summers, Ibid., 96.
55. HSCA, VI, 177.

56. Ibid.
57. Ibid.
58. Ibid.
59. The entire transcript of the Thompson interview used in Summers' film is contained in HSCA VI, ibid., 220-225.
60. Groden and Model, ibid., 1.

CHAPTER

VIII

The House
Investigates

THE HOUSE SELECT COMMITTEE ON ASSASSINATIONS left to Americans it was created to serve a marvelous heritage marked by the biggest investigative flip-flop of all time. From its inception in the fall of 1976, HSCA investigators gathered and analyzed the physical evidence in both the assassination of President Kennedy and the murder of civil rights leader Dr. Martin Luther King, Jr. During its existence, the Committee spent nearly six million dollars, required the services of more than two-hundred fifty individuals, and held more than seven weeks of public hearings. The staff conclusion was inescapable: the weight of the physical evidence in the Kennedy assassination made it clear that Lee Harvey Oswald had fired the shots that killed the President and wounded Governor Connally.

The HSCA investigation left no doubt that Oswald had acted alone. But, in the spring of 1978, a year and a half after the panel was constituted, the committee began its reversal. The reversal of the conclusions of months of hard work was based on a Dictabelt recording of Dallas Police radio channels on November 22, 1963. The HSCA in its final Report, maintained that the Dictabelt recording had captured the sound of four gunshots in Dealey Plaza, the third of which had been fired from the grassy knoll. The panel found itself in a most unusual situation. The preponderance of evidence developed for the past eighteen months had left little doubt that Oswald was the lone assassin. But the Dictabelt recordings were impressive enough for the HSCA to determine that Oswald and an unidentified conspirator had fired at the Presidential motorcade on November 22.

An elaborate acoustical reconstruction of the assassination was set up by the HSCA in Dealey Plaza. Panel members traced the source of the gunshot recordings to an open motorcycle microphone and identified a member of the police escort as the individual likely to have made the inadvertent recording. The "sound fingerprint," a unique way of measuring sound source and the resulting echo pattern, proved to the Committee and its acoustical experts that the one-gunman conclusion was, at the very least, open to serious doubt.

Before it went out of existence, the HSCA recommended that the Justice Department and the National Academy of Sciences review the acoustical evidence and report their findings. Truth to tell, both organizations did so, and discounted the finding of a probable conspiracy. Unfortunately, one was a government agency and the other relies largely on federal funds. Additionally, neither used the actual recorded evidence in their review. Accordingly, critics discounted the official findings that the acoustical analysis was invalid, and that findings of a conspiracy were unwarranted.

Since the HSCA findings discounted so many of the critics' charges regarding assassination evidence and cover-up, it is appropriate for us to examine them. And, obviously, the acoustical evidence and the tangled aftermath it provoked also demand our attention. A brief history of the HSCA is in order.

House Resolution 1540 of the 94th Congress actually served as the mandate for the House Select Committee on Assassinations. The resolution itself authorized a dozen member select committee of members of the House to investigate the assassinations of Kennedy and King, and to report its findings.[1]

Introduced a year before it was finally passed in September 1976, the resolution was actually a combination of several resolutions sponsored by some 135 members of Congress.[2] Questions sparked by Robert Groden's optically enhanced Zapruder film of the Kennedy assassination had prompted much of the congressional support for the resolution. Indeed, Congressman Thomas Downing of Virginia wrote a single-page introduction to the slim paperback authored by Groden and Pete Model. The Congressman noted that: "My introduction of the resolution . . . goes back to when I met Robert Groden and viewed, for the first time, his optically enhanced version of the motion picture of the murder. It convinced me that there was more than one assassin."[3]

What actually convinced the Congressman and his colleagues in the House was the rapid backwards movement of the President's head immediately following the fatal shot. One might pause to think that if Downing and the other 134 Congressmen had stopped to question other experts about the head snap, there might have been no House Select Committee created.

In Groden's book, Downing goes on to add that "Since that time, I have seen that film innumerable times. Robert has brought it to my office on several occasions for showing to other members of Congress. As a result, many of them have joined in our legislative record to set the record straight."[4]

Two things become apparent here. First, setting the record straight was certainly the task of the HSCA, but not everyone enjoyed the record they brought forth. Certainly, it was painful for some critics (and a few congressmen) to have their delusions of conspiracy and cover-up ripped apart before their very eyes. And second, as I mentioned in the last chapter, the call for the HSCA was based on what members of the House thought they saw in the Zapruder film, and not on what they could measure. Had I been a taxpayer at the time, I might now be upset by the less-than-careful way in which six million tax dollars were consigned to be spent.

The mandate of HR 1540 officially expired on January 3, 1977.[5] The panel had been in existence for just over three months. Three months after the demise of the Committee, House Resolution 433 gave it new life, constituting the panel for the duration of the 95th Congress. The new lease on life was to expire on January 3, 1979.[6]

Ohio Representative Louis Stokes had been named the new chairman of the Committee on March 8. Two subcommittees were created. One would investigate the assassination of President Kennedy. The other would delve into the murder of Dr. King. North Carolina Congressman Richardson Preyer was named chairman of the Kennedy subcommittee.[7] In June 1977, Professor G. Robert Blakey was appointed chief counsel and staff director. He replaced Richard Sprague, who resigned at the end of March.[8]*

---

* *Blakey subsequently wrote* The Plot to Kill the President.

The HSCA spent the next half-year deciding what to investigate and how. Indeed, the concentrated investigatory portion of the committee's lifespan covered the first seven months of 1978.[9] Public hearings were held in the last five months of the year.[10]

The critics had trouble with the panel almost from the moment of its inception. Although a veil of silence descended upon the committee's investigatory work, the critics were already reading between the lines. By the first of 1978, the Assassination Information Bureau was reporting to its newsletter readers that: "As far as we are able to discern there has been no progress. We have heard that the committee will issue an interim report in the coming weeks. Our sources caution us not to be optimistic about what this report will say."[11]

Four months later, AIB picked up a quote from Congressman Preyer that it called disturbing, adding that the comment "indicates that the committee is leaning toward the lone-gunman theory.[12] The comment by Preyer was reprinted in the May newsletter:

> "I think that from the physical, scientific, and forensic evidence we will be able to demonstrate conclusively whether or not Oswald was the lone shooter at Dealy [sic] Plaza. Of course, from the scientific evidence, you can't answer the question of whether he did have help in a conspiracy. But I think we'll be able to answer that too."[13]

The emphasis in the Preyer quote was placed there by the AIB. Elsewhere in the newsletter, the AIB quoted a *Los Angeles Times* article that maintained the HSCA investigation was "floundering badly" and would produce little in the way of new evidence.[14] Apparently, *Times* staff writers had interviewed witnesses who appeared before the HSCA in order to find source material, since the HSCA wouldn't divulge much to the press. The AIB newsletter quotes the *Times* article as saying that: "The committee and its investigators have labored mightily to unearth conspiracies in both cases—but to no avail."[15]

Now, my reasoning may be a bit flawed, but it strikes me that if an honest, fact-finding panel composed of elected members of the United States Congress can't locate a conspiracy, that probably means there wasn't one to begin with. Indeed, midway through the HSCA investigation the critics seemed to say, "Who cares about the evidence you people have studied . . . the witnesses you've talked to . . . we don't care what all your work shows. We just want another assassin."

The legion of Warren Report detractors, who had urged this new investigation in the first place, seemed prepared to wash their hands of the entire affair even before the HSCA went into public hearings. After the fourth day of public hearings in August 1978, Harold Weisberg told me that the committee was "being very selective about what they present."[16]

Unknown to the critics, the committee was prepared to throw them and the American people a sop of sorts. Dallas Police Dictabelt recordings of channels one and two at the time of the assassination were located and obtained by the committee's investigators in March, 1978.[17] Two months later, the committee contracted with the Cambridge, Massachusetts, firm of Bolt, Beranek and Newman, Inc., to perform an acoustical analysis of the DPD materials.[18]

After screening the channel one tape and determining that there were, in fact, impulse patterns present that may have been assassination gunfire, BBN recommended an on-site test in Dealey Plaza. Tape recordings there could then be matched with the sounds recorded on the Dictabelt.[19] As the committee noted in its report:

> *"The echo patterns in a complex environment such as Dealey Plaza are unique, so by conducting the reconstruction, the committee could obtain unique 'acoustical fingerprints' of various shooter, target, and microphone locations. The fingerprint's identifying characteristic would be the unique time-spacing between the echoes. If any of the acoustical fingerprints produced in the 1978 reconstruction matched those on the 1963 Dallas police dispatch tape, it would be a strong indication that the sounds on the 1963 Dallas police dispatch tape were caused by gunfire recorded by a police microphone in Dealey Plaza."[20]*

Acoustic reconstruction of the assassination was conducted by the committee on Sunday, August 20, 1978. Placing sandbags at four locations in the middle of Elm Street that approximated the position of the Presidential limousine, the committee asked marksmen to fire from two locations: the sixth-floor window of the Depository, and behind the wooden fence atop the grassy knoll. An array of microphones was arranged to record the sounds of gunfire. Dozens of microphones were placed along Houston Street, since the committee did not know where the police microphone was when it recorded the sounds on the November 22, 1963, Dictabelt.

The firing began before sun-up. It lasted through the noon hour. Those of us standing across Dealey Plaza were impressed by various things. I was most impressed by the lack of attention to detail and the almost casual attitude toward the reconstruction taken by the scientific "experts" who were conducting it.

First, there were no boxes on the sixth floor. Readers may remember that the assassin fired from the southeast corner window of the Depository after stacking up carton upon carton of books behind and above him to shield himself from view. Now, I'm not an audio expert, but it occurs to me that the rifle blast might just as easily echo off those book cartons as the buildings and structures in the plaza below. Were I trying to match echo "fingerprints," I would certainly have included boxes behind the gunman.

Second, there was no train on the triple overpass as there was at the moment of the actual assassination. Since the shots were being fired down Elm Street toward the underpass itself, I would have thought that the train atop the bridge would have been yet another source of echoes. It was apparently not taken into account.

Third, two different types of ammunition were used. Down in the plaza, we could hear a distinct difference when the riflemen switched from one type to the next. Again, one would think that sounds differing to the human ear would produce differing echo patterns. The scientific community didn't bother to take this into account.

Finally, only two assassin locations, the Depository and the wooden fence atop the grassy knoll, had been selected for the reconstruction. This selectivity lessened the chances that another sound fingerprint would be found to match those on the Dictabelt.

Experts who reviewed the results of the reenactment and the original Dictabelt were fifty-fifty on the question of a second gunman. Since there was no other physical evidence to indicate the presence of another assassin, the Committee decided to draft a final report that indicated no conspiracy had existed. But then Chief Counsel Blakey found two additional acoustic experts who maintained that they were 95 percent certain that a fourth shot had been fired from the grassy knoll.

Testifying before the panel, both Mark Weiss and Ernest Aschkenasy swore that they understood the historical significance of their finding.

Committee staffers had determined that the original Dictabelt recording was probably made by a police motorcycle radio which was inadvertently stuck open. They traced the motorcycle indicated in the acoustical reenactment to officer H.B. McLain, whom they called to Washington to testify.[21] Incredibly, McLain was not given the opportunity to listen to the Dictabelt tape before or after his testimony.

Counsel Blakey dismissed this crucial omission by claiming that McLain hadn't asked to review the audio recording![22]Significant in this omission, however, is the fact that the tape contains no sounds of sirens turning on immediately after the assassination, as the motorcade and its police escort sped to Parkland Hospital. It does contain the sound of sirens approaching and then receding at about two minutes after the supposed shots were recorded. Thus, it would appear that the microphone was along the motorcade route in a stationary position, rather than moving.[23] Officer McLain, hearing the tape subsequent to his HSCA testimony, claimed that the originating motorcycle could not have been his.[24] Predictably, Blakey refused to recall him as a witness.[25]

Not being a scientist, I will defer to the conclusion of those who are, that the wave patterns recorded during the 1978 reenactment do indeed match those recorded on the Dictabelt. But I did witness the reenactment, and it was not a faithful re-creation of the assassination. I put great stock in the denial of Officer McLain. The Dictabelt, then, is a paradox. It apparently is what it cannot be.

Another serious problem arises when the wave patterns representing shots on the Dictabelt are compared to the clock represented by the Zapruder film. The HSCA went backward and forward trying to find a match; there is none to be found. However, in an effort to shore up the two-gunman thesis, the Committee advanced in the final report a four-shot time-line which included a third shot from the grassy knoll:

Impulse Pattern and Source	*Corresponds to Z-Frame*
One *(Texas School Book Depository)*	*157-161*
Two *(Texas School Book Depository)*	*188-191*
Three *(The Grassy Knoll)*	*295-296*
Four *(Texas School Book Depository)*	*312*

Difficulties exist with the HSCA time-line. The HSCA reconstruction creates a three-second gap between when President Kennedy and Governor Connally were wounded and when the governor, who was shot through the chest, shows signs of injury. Furthermore, Oswald's rifle required about 2.3 seconds between shots without allowing time for aiming. But based on the fact that Zapruder's camera ran at 18.3 frames per second, the interval between the first shot and the second shot was 1.6 seconds. This fact would argue for another gunman firing from the same location. To skirt this point, the Committee suggested that Oswald had used the open-iron sights on his Carcano rather than the telescopic sight. While I'm not at all uncomfortable with this thought, the time interval should still have been longer.

By far the biggest problem facing the HSCA was the question of the second gunman atop the knoll. No physical evidence suggested that another assassin existed. Add to the lack of proof the HSCA finding that the shot from the knoll apparently missed. To have a trained gunman miss a cross-shot from a distance of 110 feet is not out of the realm of possibility. What is beyond the frame of serious thought is that the gunman fired a bullet that not only missed the President, the other five occupants of the auto, and the limousine itself, striking nothing despite its downward trajectory. In a word, the bullet disappeared. Still, the Committee's four-shot sequence insisted on a third shot in its sequence of four being fired from the grassy knoll by a gunman no one saw, who apparently wasn't proficient at his task and used disappearing bullets.*

Not once in its final report did the HSCA address how a gunman firing from the knoll might have missed, nor did it speculate on where the bullet hit. Having rushed to judgment on the issue of the Dictabelt and what the recording showed, the Committee dissolved itself with the admonition that it was unable to identify the other gunman and that the Department of Justice should examine the audio evidence to see if it concurred with the Committee's findings.

Of course, the Justice Department did not concur, nor did the National Academy of Sciences. The NAS review, in particular, discovered the existence of "bleedover" on the Dictabelt at the time of the

---

Understandably, Blakey stayed with this absurd line of reasoning because he had forthcoming book royalties at stake.

assassination. This bleedover contained dialogue between law enforcement officers that indicated the portion of the recording where shots
were found had actually been recorded a minute or so after the
assassination.

Since neither the Department of Justice nor the NAS felt con-
strained to listen to the original Dictabelt before refuting the HSCA
conclusions, some critics have attacked their evidence as well as the
results of the studies themselves. Robert Groden and Gary Mack, in
particular, claim that a sixty-cycle tone on the Dictabelt copy used by the
NAS indicates that it had been re-dubbed, meaning that the channel two
"bleedover" had been deliberately recorded over the sound of shots on
channel one.[26]

I would expect this sort of tampering-with-the-evidence cry from
Groden. But Mack is a television producer and should know better. I
certainly do, having spent seven long years as a disc jockey. A sixty-
cycle tone generates whenever a copy of a recording is made, and is
accounted for in this case by the fact that the evidence examined by the
NAS and the Department of Justice is a copy of the original and not the
original itself. The tone in and of itself is no indication of tampering.
Interestingly, neither Groden nor Mack have ever bothered to check the
original Dictabelt to see if the bleedover appears on the actual evidence
examined by the HSCA. It does, not just once, but several times.[27] The
Dictabelt evidence, then, is neither fish nor fowl, and in our quest for the
truth must be viewed as inadmissible. I'd be more inclined to agree with
the HSCA findings if there was medical evidence or physical damage
to indicate that the gunman firing from atop the knoll had actually hit
something. I've stood behind that fence too long and too often to believe
in a point-blank miss.

I remain unconvinced that Officer McLain was operating the
motorcycle with the stuck microphone. McLain, some distance behind
the President, should have picked up his own siren when he switched
it on immediately after the assassination. The Dictabelt recording has no
close-range sound of sirens. Groden's assertion that the gain control
(AGC) in the radio circuit prevented the siren from being heard is
absurd. The purpose of an AGC is not to obliterate sounds, but rather
to hold them to a manageable level. The siren would have been heard

on the tape as well as other loud sounds nearby.[28]

The problem that remains is explaining why the sound finger-prints on the Dictabelt match those recorded during the reconstruction in Dealey Plaza. To be candid, they don't. The HSCA Report admits that the matching standards were arranged on a point basis, since the odds of obtaining an exact match were very slim. The sound fingerprints matched well enough for the Committee's purposes, but to say (as Groden does again and again) that they were unique to Dealey Plaza is stretching the truth.[29]

Dallas-based researcher Mary Ferrell, who brought the Dictabelt to the attention of the HSCA, told me in the summer of 1988 that, despite presenting it to the Committee, she herself had never believed in the validity of the acoustical evidence.*

In all fairness, the HSCA did produce some worthwhile conclu-sions, despite the fatal flaw of giving credence to the Dictabelt record-ing. As I mentioned in the previous chapter, the panel's photographic analysis rendered a valuable service to both the critics and the American public. And the forensic analysis was among the best work the Commit-tee turned out.

Indeed, one must keep in mind that the panel had found and had been ready to support the conclusion that Lee Oswald, acting alone, killed both Officer Tippit and President Kennedy. All of the physical evidence led to this conclusion, no matter how disappointing it was to the critics who had fomented the investigation. Only the discovery of the Dictabelt evidence and Chief Counsel Blakey's gerrymandering of the related expert opinion and testimony kept the Committee from issuing its no-conspiracy conclusion.

In his ability to control the final report of his committee, Blakey must be regarded as something of a historical wizard. When the panel reached conclusions he didn't share, no matter how well documented and supported those conclusions were, Blakey became a magician in a business suit. Waving his magic wand, he declared the no-conspiracy conclusion null and void, basing his refutation on, in my view, the flimsiest of evidence. When the Committee folded its tent, Blakey went

---

* Mrs. Ferrell is a genuine paradox among researchers. Having studied the case since 1963, she had never been to the sixth floor until Project Director Conover Hunt took her there in 1988.

on to publish a book and profit from the new, unsupported conclusions he had so skillfully engineered. The multi-assassin theory was indispensable to Blakey, given his natural bias. The Chief Counsel credits organized crime with the assassination, despite the fact that there isn't a shred of hard, cold evidence to link the mob to the crime.

In his latest book, *Final Disclosure*, former Warren Commission counsel David Belin writes that Blakey ". . . and his staff succeeded in their efforts behind closed doors to convince a majority of the committee at the last moment that the invisible second gunman corroborated Blakey's theory that Jack Ruby stalked Lee Harvey Oswald from the hours immediately after the assassination until he killed Oswald on the Sunday morning following the assassination."[30]

In writing *The Plot to Kill the President*, Blakey and co-author Dick Billings were attempting to write the perfect epitaph to the HSCA investigation. And they almost succeeded. After all, what reviewer or critic would defend organized crime? And who would defend the dead Jack Ruby? Belin continues:

"If there had been public hearings on Blakey's theory, the allegations of Ruby's involvement in a conspiracy could never have been sustained because of the overwhelming evidence to the contrary and in particular the testimony of Rabbi Hillel Silverman, who visited Ruby in the Dallas County jail once or twice a week and became extremely close to him."[31]

Silverman had told Belin following the Warren Commission investigation that Ruby was absolutely innocent of any conspiracy to murder the President.[32]

Blakey, however, insists that Ruby's killing of Oswald bore all the signs of an organized crime hit.[33] Since when do organized crime figures gun down a man held in police custody while he is walking through a crowded police department basement and in plain view of millions of television viewers? My research leads me to believe that only in Professor Blakey's mind did Ruby kill Oswald to silence him.

In the early 1980s, while a disc jockey in Arkansas, I met a man who had retired from the Marcello organization in New Orleans. During several conversations, this individual told me that the assassination and the killing of Oswald were acts independent of organized crime. This person told me several times that real mafia hits don't occur in a crowded plaza or in the police department basement.

Further relegating Professor Blakey's misguided efforts to the junk pile of history is his dependence on the acoustical evidence for the second-gunman conclusion. Prior to the NAS and Justice Department review of the evidence, Blakey wrote to the *National Review*:

> *"The Department of Justice has announced that it is going to verify the acoustics testing done by the House Assassinations Committee. I assume it will be done with competency and integrity. If so, I will abide by its results. If it indicates that there is not a 95% probability that there was a gunshot from the grassy knoll, I will write a letter to the* Review *and withdraw all that I have said."* [34]

You have read that the NAS and the Justice Department flatly discounted the second-gunman conclusion. As you might guess, the *National Review* is still waiting to hear from Professor Blakey.

I hope they don't hold their breath.

1. HSCA, *Report*, 9.
2. Ibid.
3. Groden and Model, 1.
4. Ibid.
5. HSCA, *Report*, 9.
6. Ibid., 10.
7. Ibid.
8. Ibid.
9. Ibid., 18.
10. Ibid., 19.
11. AIB *Newsletter*, January/February 1978.
12. AIB *Newsletter*, May/June 1978.
13. Ibid., source *United Press International*.
14. Ibid.
15. Ibid.
16. Conversation with Weisberg, August 15, 1978.
17. HSCA, *Report*, 67.
18. Ibid., 66.
19. Ibid., 68.
20. Ibid., 69.
21. Ibid., 71.
22. David W. Belin, *Final Disclosure*, (New York: Scribner's, 1988), 192.
23. Ibid., 191.
24. Ibid.
25. Ibid.
26. Groden and Livingstone, *High Treason*, 223.
27. Belin, 199.
28. Groden and Livingstone, 215.
29. Ibid.
30. Belin, 195.
31. Ibid., 196.
32. Ibid., 37.
33. Ibid., 196.
34. Ibid., 203.

IX

The President's Back and Neck Wounds

READERS WHO POSSESS SOME KNOWLEDGE OF THE ASSASSINATION will probably believe that the first shot to hit President Kennedy resulted in a wound from which he would have eventually recovered, had not a subsequent shot hit his skull. This misconception is shared by writers such as William Manchester, who declared in his *Death of a President:* "The President was wounded, but not fatally. A 6.5 millimeter bullet had entered the back of his neck, bruised his lung, ripped his windpipe and exited at his throat, nicking the knot of his tie."[1]

Manchester's assertion aside, the back-to-throat wound was not one from which Mr. Kennedy would likely have recovered without incident. Dr. John Lattimer, discussing the injury in his book, *Kennedy and Lincoln*, maintains that Kennedy would have faced an uphill recovery ". . . his chances for survival would have been affected unfavorably by that first bullet alone."[2]

It should be remembered that the Parkland doctors who worked in vain to save the President's life saw only the wounds in Kennedy's throat and head. The only exception was Dr. Marion T. Jenkins, who in performing his duties as anesthesiologist, brushed his fingers over the back wound.[3] Of course, Dr. Malcolm Perry chose (properly so) to obliterate the hole in the President's throat by using the site for a tracheotomy.[4]

Dr. Perry did not communicate with the doctors who performed the autopsy on the President's body until the day after the assassination. Thus, the doctors at Bethesda did not know, and could only surmise, that the site of the tracheotomy also marked the site of a bullet wound.

Indeed, the autopsy surgeons spent considerable time probing the wound in the President's back to determine the course of the missile.

Strap muscles in the neck blocked the path of their surgical probes. The surgeons were denied permission to dissect the track of the bullet, presumably because officials were anxious to avoid any further disfigurement of the President's body.[5]

This quandary led critics such as Dr. Josiah Thompson and Edward Jay Epstein to conclude that the Warren Report's depiction of the President's "non-fatal" wounds was a combination of fabrication and distortion. The critics relied on an inaccurate report by FBI agents Sibert and O'Neill which maintained that a bullet had hit the President " just below his shoulder to the right of the spinal column."[6] The December 9, 1963, FBI Summary Report added that the bullet ranged "at an angle of 45 to 60 degrees downward, that there was no point of exit and that the bullet was not in the body."[7]

Using the early FBI document as their foundation for speculation, the critics maintained that some sort of "low velocity" shot must have hit the President in the shoulder, penetrated only a few inches, and fallen out onto his stretcher at Parkland Hospital. There are myriad problems contained within the critics' hypothesis. First, the bullet found at Parkland Hospital most likely came from Governor Connally's stretcher, not the President's; although the critics went out of their way to prove that it could have been either one.

Second, it's hard to imagine a bullet with such little penetrating power that it would advance only a few inches into soft tissue and then stop. In *Six Seconds in Dallas*, Josiah Thompson describes this cartridge as a "'short charge'—that is, a cartridge whose explosive power was far less than standard."[8]

Unfortunately, Thompson has no evidence from which to deduce that the bullet which struck President Kennedy in the back was, in fact, fired from a cartridge loaded with a so-called "short charge." Indeed, the short charge is merely one more supposition presented by the good doctor for which no supporting evidence exists.

Still more unlikely, Thompson concludes that the wound in the President's throat was caused by a fragment of bone driven down through the cranial vault and neck by the explosive power of the shot which struck the President in the head.

The arguments advanced by the critics in the late 1960s are now academic. Today we possess what they did not have—a careful, thorough and unbiased review of the photographs and x-rays of the body of President Kennedy. Without them, the critics were flying blind (and were apparently content to make the best of it).

Admittedly, projectile tracks through soft tissue like that of the neck are difficult to read. But when you're confronted with an entry wound in the shoulder, and another wound at the throat, it doesn't take a genius to determine that a single bullet traversed the neck area.

A closer look at the President's first injuries raises some troubling questions that begin to appear through the chain of evidence. The President was struck in the upper back, just below the juncture of the neck and the back.[9] The wound measured about six by eight millimeters in size, roughly a quarter of an inch longer across than up and down.[10] There was a "halo" around the rim—a blackened edge that suggested strongly that this was a wound of entry.[11] As we will see, there is little else it could have been.

Critics have maintained through the years that the wound in the President's back was situated too low for the bullet which caused it to exit from his throat, given a downward angle from Oswald's vantage point in the Book Depository. They overlooked two things. First, the President had more soft tissue about the back of his neck than do most individuals.[12] This lowered the position of the back wound when his body was measured on the autopsy table, since the area around the back and shoulders tends to rise when sitting (or riding in an automobile) and fall when lying flat on the back or stomach. Second, the critics ignore the fact that the autopsy face sheets (schematic drawings—which constituted the only evidence critics had for years) were crudely drawn and not intended to represent actual wound locations. The location of the back wound on the face sheet is shown considerably lower than the corresponding wound in the throat and the extra roll of tissue around Kennedy's neck is not mentioned.*

Had the process been reversed—the throat wound one of entry and the back wound one of exit—there would surely have been some damage to the seat or trunk of the Presidential limousine. Of course,

---

* Most critics have now abandoned any conjecture that a shot from the front caused the throat wound. An exception is Robert Groden, who claims the autopsy photos and x-rays are forgeries.

there was none.

A significant problem belabored by the critics arises when one carefully examines the clothing worn by the President when he was shot. Here, an entirely different set of variables comes into play. The neck wound is simple enough—two slits near the collar button and a nick in the lining of the President's tie. As we'll see, the very location of these holes in the President's shirt answers another question the critics have raised.

The difficulty lies with the President's jacket. This lightweight, grey fabric suit coat is another silent key to the assassination riddle. A roundish, punched-in, quarter-inch hole is just more than thirteen centimeters below the upper edge of the collar, and some 4.5 centimeters to the right of the midline. Its position is somewhat lower than the corresponding wound on the President's back.

Since the back of the President's shirt shows a six-by-six millimeter hole in the jacket, the mute evidence seems to indicate a lower point of entry than would be possible if the bullet had been fired from above and behind, and had coursed through the President's neck to exit at his throat.

The critics pounced upon this very tangible (and silent) evidence with obvious joy. Through the years, there have been several attempts to justify the position of the clothing holes with the entry wound on the President's back. These attempts were made principally by defenders of the Warren Report who, like the critics, overlooked crucial evidence with a negative bearing on their contentions.

A good example is the hypothesis first advanced by Dr. Lattimer and published in *Kennedy and Lincoln*. Dr. Lattimer, confronted with the low position of the holes in the clothing, realized the problem at hand and went back to the drawing board:

> *"Having seen these holes in the back of the coat and shirt, at their low locations, I returned to my file of Kennedy photographs and found several of the President taken shortly before he was shot, with his right elbow resting on the edge of the automobile, where he could wave more easily. This position caused his suit coat to hump up on the back of his neck. It was easy to see that the bullet hole in the coat or shirt might well be at a lower point on either garment when the garment was laid out flat, in comparison to its position*

at the actual moment of impact when President Kennedy was indeed waving to the crowds, with his right elbow elevated." [13]

Time magazine writer Ed Magnuson clearly had Lattimer's research at hand when he wrote in a 1975 article that: "Since Kennedy was seen in the Zapruder film to be waving before he was first struck in the back of the neck, the experts believe that his raised right arm bunched up the top of the jacket; unfolded, the jacket thus shows a hole lower than the one in his back."[14]

The article included a convenient diagram so that readers could see the obvious plausibility of the bunched-jacket theory. The problem with Lattimer's argument is not in the theory itself, but rather, in the photos he used as reference. The picture published in his book was taken from the motorcade's press bus, very likely at the outset or in the first minutes of the procession from Love Field.

Two other photos exist (both readily available to Lattimer) showing the President's back at the time of the first shot. These, then, would be much better evidence than one showing his jacket bunched at the beginning of the motorcade. The photos taken at the moment of the assassination were a color slide by Phil Willis and a black-and-white still by Hugh Betzner. Both were shot from the south curb of Elm Street, and both depict the back of President Kennedy's head, since the limousine has already passed both photographers and is headed down the slope of Elm Street. Also visible in both photographs are the President's shoulders and upper back. The Betzner photo clearly shows the President's shirt collar, which would not be visible were his jacket bunched. Although not as evident in the Willis slide, the collar is also detectable and the jacket appears flat.

There is another problem with Lattimer's explanation, although it requires some thought up-front. Were it not for the photographic evidence, I could accept the theory of the bunched suit jacket. But what about a bunched shirt? Hardly possible, since the President's shirts were custom-made and carefully fitted. Indeed, the law of averages also works against Lattimer, for in his scenario, the shirt would have to be bunched inside the jacket almost to the same degree as the coat. The odds against this millimeter-for-millimeter correspondence boggle the imagination.

Obviously, a bullet fired from above and behind would not enter the President's back and, striking no bone, deflect itself upward to exit his throat. The suit and shirt bullet holes must be correct and must correspond with the wound visible on the President's body. But how?

The answer, revealed in more detail later, is that the President was already reacting to a shot when the bullet struck him in the right shoulder. Leaning forward with his hands in front of his face, his suit, jacket, and shirt were both elevated, thus accounting for the differing positions of the wound in his back when compared with the holes in his clothing. Although this hints at my final solution it demands presentation here.

The critics have had a field day with the descriptions of the President's throat wound given by the Dallas doctors. At Parkland, physicians had their only opportunity to examine the neck wound. Before it was obliterated by Dr. Perry's tracheotomy, the wound exuded bloody air bubbles. In *Kennedy and Lincoln* Dr. Lattimer notes that Dr. Perry described the wounds "only about one-fourth inch in diameter."[15] Lattimer goes on to add that:

> "*Some critics of the Warren Report seized upon this fact (Perry's comment) indicating that it must have been a wound of entry rather than a wound of exit, as the Commission had concluded. It is, of course, true that 6.5mm fully-jacketed military Carcano bullets of the type that killed Kennedy usually makes a much larger wound of exit than of entrance, in unsupported skin.*"[16]

Although Josiah Thompson argues with great vagueness that the slits in President Kennedy's shirt collar were caused by a bone fragment,[17] and though the shirt fabric was strangely without traces of metal,* most critics are forced by common sense to agree that the holes in the shirt collar were caused by a bullet.

A bullet entering the President's throat would have to exit from the President's back. Since there was no damage either to the seat back, the trunk of the automobile, or the follow-up car we can logically assume that the throat wound is one of exit. Having established what it is, let's

---

* *The holes in the back of Kennedy's jacket did reveal minute traces of copper, which comprised the jacket of Oswald's ammunition.*

turn our attention to Dr. Lattimer's unanswered question: why wasn't the throat wound bigger?

During a press conference on the afternoon of the assassination, newsmen asked Dr. Perry if, since the throat wound was so small, it might have been a wound of entrance. Perry correctly answered that it could have been either an entrance or an exit. He had no knowledge of the circumstances of the assassination, and fielded the question the best he could. Since we know that the wound had to be one of exit, why did it not appear bigger in dimension?

Lattimer does a good job of explaining the small wound:

> *"The bullet left the front of the President's neck, turning slightly nose-down, as I saw it, creating half-inch-long vertical slits in this shirt immediately below and touching the collar band just at the bullet hole. The President's challis necktie was also in place, giving further support for the skin of the area. There was a bloodstain on the knot where blood was carried from the neck out onto the necktie."* [18]

In a word, the President's shirt collar and tie held the skin surface tightly enough that the bullet, though it might have been tumbling slightly, did not have an opportunity to produce its characteristically larger exit wound. The President's necktie, in and of itself, could not have added much rigidity to the skin structure of his neck because of the type and manufacture of the tie. Kennedy was wearing a Christian Dior Challis tie, a very lightweight, thin piece of neckwear. The knot of the tie, however, was in exactly the correct position to add the support Dr. Lattimer postulates necessary for the small exit wound. I'm inclined to accept his theory as accurate.

Indeed, Dr. Lattimer and his sons performed some eerily realistic mock-up experiments to simulate the effects of Kennedy's necktie and shirt collar on the size of the exit wound. They discovered that, as the collar support was moved further away from the wound site, the wound itself became correspondingly larger. [19]

You'll recall my rather mysterious claim that President Kennedy was already reacting to a shot when he was struck in the back. Obviously, with hands raised to face-level, bent slightly forward, the shirt collar would have been tightly in place about his neck. This, again, is food for thought in a later chapter.

Strangely, the House Select Committee skirted the issue of the small throat wound, indicating only that its Medical and Firearms Panel agreed that the slits in the President's shirt collar were characteristic of bullet exit wounds. In two other paragraphs, the Panel concluded that Dr. Lattimer's theory was probably the correct explanation:

> "The panel members agree that the fabric of the shirt and tie and their anatomic relationship to the underlying missile wound might have served as sufficient reinforcement to diminish distortion of the skin. Several panel members are also of the opinion that an unshored exit wound of a missile of comparable size and velocity might be similar if the missile were not misshapen by striking a substantial bone within the body."[20]

Interestingly, the HSCA published a fine sketch in *Volume VII* which depicted the President leaning forward at the time he was struck in the upper back.[21] This position accounted for not only the constricted shirt collar and tie knot, but the upraised coat and shirt backs as well. There *is* a problem with the HSCA drawing as it depicts the bullet trajectory from Oswald's rifle. The HSCA, you'll remember, maintains that Kennedy was hit in the back prior to passing behind the roadway sign which blocked him from view in the Zapruder film. Kennedy is thus clearly visible. He is not leaning forward.*

Taking into account the slope of Elm Street, my on-site tests lead me to believe that the bullet which struck the President in the shoulder entered at an angle of 19 degrees 42 minutes, and followed a nearly straight high path through his neck. The House Select Committee, on the other hand, postulated a wound with an angle of about 24 degrees. Again, this distortion of the known medical findings reflects the Committee's willingness to manipulate the data in order to accommodate the acoustical evidence necessary to support a conspiracy finding. Since the President was leaning forward when he was first hit, the angle of the bullet through his shoulder and neck would be lessened to some degree. Just as the angle of the bullet through Governor Connally's body increased because he was leaning somewhat backward when struck, so the angle of the bullet through the President's back and throat decreased because he was tilted forward at the moment of impact.

---

* This is still more evidence that the HSCA altered the entire scope of their investigation with the last-minute acceptance of the acoustical evidence.

The HSCA managed to ignore altogether the inconsistencies involved in having the President first wounded as early as frame 190. Indeed, the panel maintained that the entrance and exit wounds for the back-through-throat shot were about level.[22] Then, the Committee had Tom Canning, a trajectory analyst with an impressive NASA background, review the Zapruder film frames and, from the photographic record, determine the timing of the first wounding shot and the position of the President when the bullet struck. Canning's often highly technical testimony took great pains to explain how he arrived at the conclusion that the President was wounded before Kennedy disappeared from the view of Zapruder's movie camera:

> "His right shoulder appears to be slightly elevated relative to his left, as determined from Zapruder's pictures, between frames 160 and 200. We include the wound position data interpreted from the forensic pathologist report as modified to account for the change in the President's posture and movement of his torso. The resulting difference in height of his back and neck wounds relative to the car gives us the slope relative to the car. Then we place the car on the sloping street in Dealey Plaza and maintain this same angular relationship between this line labeled "To Gun" in the exhibit and the line along the side of the limousine body."[23]

The problem with Canning's deductions lies in the fact that were the President wounded in the back at about frame 190, he would have reacted almost immediately. No doubt he would have been acutely aware of the pain of the entering and exiting bullet. Yet, the President continues to stare straight ahead through the last frame in which he is visible prior to disappearing behind the road sign. That frame is 207. Since Zapruder's camera ran at roughly 18 frames per second, Canning would have us believe that the President was wounded but showed no reaction for at least a second after he had been shot through the throat.

The only other possibility is that the President, in frames 190 through 207, is reacting to the sound of a missed shot. Such an event would have undoubtedly confused him, and caused a delay in his reaction time. The HSCA, because it wanted so badly to synchronize the Zapruder film with the acoustic record, ignored this possibility and focused instead on an inexplicable "delayed reaction" for President Kennedy and for Governor Connally as well! When the President reappears from behind the road sign in the Zapruder film, his hands rise in a rapid, covering motion to just above chin-level. Indeed, his right hand appears to touch the ridge of his nose by frame 235, while his left hand, continuing to rise, is directly beneath his right. The President would seem to be responding more to a facial injury than to a bullet that had just transited his neck. The President is also leaning markedly forward in the frames immediately after he comes back into view. This forward torso movement continues until the fatal head shot explodes his right temple.

After Governor Connally appears to have been wounded (his cheeks expand, his right shoulder drops dramatically and his hair is mussed), Kennedy's hands do drop to clutch at his throat. But prior to the moment when the Governor shows obvious pain, the President keeps his hands in front of the lower half of his face. It's important to remember that at no time in frames 235 to 238 do either of Kennedy's hands cover his neck or throat.

To sum up, it appears likely that the President was hit by a bullet moving with a downward declination of about 19 degrees 42 minutes, and that shot struck him in the right shoulder. Hunched forward at the time, Kennedy's body position allowed the bullet to travel an almost level path through his body and exit his throat, passing through his stiff shirt collar and nicking the knot of his thin necktie.

While the Warren Commission concluded that the President could have been struck any time between frames 210 and 225 of the Zapruder film, the HSCA determined to its own satisfaction that he was probably hit by the second of the four impulses on the Dictabelt recording. Since the moment of the headshot could be most accurately matched to the Dictabelt, the panel was then forced to conclude that the President was hit before he disappeared behind the road sign, most likely in the vicinity of frame 190. As we have seen, the HSCA conclusion does not fit the photographic evidence used to support it.

In its effort to gerrymander the evidence to fit Blakey's pro-conspiracy conclusions, the panel was forced to conclude that the President suffered a delayed reaction to his gunshot wound on the order of two seconds or more, and that his body position at about frame 190 was sufficiently hunched forward for the bullet to have taken an almost level course through his neck. As we have seen, the President was not in the correct position to have been wounded in the back prior to frame 230. Oddly enough, the HSCA's own drawings, when compared to the Zapruder film frames, confirm this and clearly indicate that the panel was in error as to the timing of the first shot.

Now, let's examine the injuries suffered by the other gentleman shot that day in Dealey Plaza.

I. Manchester, 156.
2. Lattimer, 245.
3. Ibid.,153.
4. Ibid., 201.
5. Ibid., 156.
6. Epstein, *Inquest*, 59.
7. Ibid.
8. Thompson, 221.
9. Lattimer, 198.
10. Ibid., 200.
11. Ibid.
12. Ibid., 203.
13. Ibid., 204.
14. *Time*, November 24, 1975, 34.
15. Lattimer, 230.
16. Ibid.
17. Thompson, 64.
18. Lattimer, 231.
19. Ibid., 235.
20. HSCA, VII, Page 95
21. Ibid., 100.
22. HSCA, II, 170.
23. Ibid., 178.

X

The Governor's Wounds

UNLIKE PRESIDENT KENNEDY'S BACK AND THROAT WOUNDS, the questions surrounding the wounding of Governor Connally are clearer and somewhat easier to understand. Since the Governor survived and is alive today, it's not so much a question of where he was struck by the assassin's bullet, but when and how.

Connally was riding directly in front of the President. He and his wife, Nellie, were sitting on folding jump seats located between the back seat, where the President and Mrs. Kennedy sat, and the back of the front seat, where the Secret Service driver and escort rode. Nearly a week after the assassination, Governor Connally told the *New York Times* that

> *"We heard a shot. I turned to my left. I was sitting in the jump seat. I turned to my left in the back seat. The President had slumped. He had said nothing. Almost simultaneously, as I turned, I was hit, and I knew I'd been hit badly, and I said I knew the President had been hit—and I said, "My God, they're not going to kill us all."*[1]

On April 21, 1964, the Governor testified before the Warren Commission. Questioned by Assistant Counsel Arlen Specter, Connally gave this description of the events on November 22:

> *"We had just made the turn, well, when I heard what I thought was a shot. I heard this noise which I immediately took to be a rifle shot. I instinctively turned to my right because the sound appeared to come from over my right shoulder, and I saw nothing unusual except just people in the crowd, but I did not catch the President in the corner of my eye, and I was interested because once I heard the shot in my own mind I identified it as a rifle shot, and I immediately—the only thought that crossed my mind was that this*

is an assassination attempt.

"So I looked, failing to see him, I was turning to look back over my left shoulder into the back seat, but I never got that far in my turn. I got about in the position I am now facing you, looking a little bit to the left of center, and then I felt like someone hit me in the back."[2]

The Governor has remained remarkably consistent in his recollections of the assassination. Unfortunately for the Warren Commission and the House Select Committee, a large part of their case for a lone assassin depended upon the Governor having been mistaken about what transpired during those fateful few seconds.

Assistant Counsel Specter asked the Governor which bullet had caused his injury. Connally replied that it had been the second shot. Apparently unsatisfied with that answer, Specter asked the Governor to elaborate on his reasoning. The Governor answered:

"Well, in my judgment, it just couldn't conceivably been the first one because I heard the sound of the shot. In the first place, I don't know anything about the velocity of this particular bullet, but any rifle has a velocity that exceeds the speed of sound, and when I heard the sound of that first shot, that bullet had already reached where I was or it had reached that far, and after I heard that shot, I had the time to turn to my right, and start to turn to my left before I felt anything."[3]

Connally, it should be noted, did not hear the second shot, the shot he claims wounded him. Rather, he believes that he heard only the first and third reports.[4] The Governor correctly stated that the bullets from Oswald's rifle traveled faster than the speed of sound, so the bullet which did indeed strike Connally was already embedded in the Governor's thigh before the sound of the shot reached the limousine. Connally testified that since he didn't hear the second shot, he believed that it was the bullet which wounded him.[5] As I mentioned, this was not what the Warren Commission wanted to hear.

Having studied the Zapruder Film, the Commission staff believed that President Kennedy was reacting to a bullet wound by the time he was again visible coming from behind the roadway sign. As we will see, this conclusion was in error. The difficulty arose because the Governor has clearly been hit by frame 240, a maximum of only thirty frames after Oswald's view of the limousine was no longer blocked by the large oak tree at frame 210. With the Zapruder camera running at 18.3 frames per second, thirty frames would have represented less than two seconds of running time. And Oswald's Carcano required 2.3 seconds between shots, assuming the rifleman had used the telescopic sight.

The Commission, therefore, decided that the Governor unintentionally had been mistaken in his testimony. It ascribed a delayed reaction to the Governor in an effort to explain why he appeared unhurt at least a half-second and as much as a second and a half after the President had been hit. The Warren Report stated that:

"In evaluating the films in the light of these timing guides, it was kept in mind that a victim of a bullet wound may not react immediately, and, in some situations, according to experts, the victim may not even know where he has been hit, or when."[6]

The Governor believed that he knew immediately that he had been struck by the shot. He told the Warren Commission that the impact was substantial: "I would say it is as if someone doubled his fist and came up behind you and just with a 12-inch blow hit you right in the back right below the shoulder blade."[7]

The Warren Report, however, maintained that: "There was, conceivably, a delayed reaction between the time the bullet struck him and the time he realized that he was hit, despite the fact that the bullet struck a glancing blow to a rib and penetrated his wrist bone."[8] In brief, the bullet struck Governor Connally in the back beneath the right shoulder blade, collapsed a lung and broke his fifth rib as it passed through his chest, exited the chest beneath the right nipple, completely shattered his right wrist and embedded itself in his thigh. The Commission and later, the HSCA would have us believe that those injuries would not be severe enough for the Governor to immediately realize that he had been struck.

Governor Connally himself studied the Zapruder film and picked frame 234 as the moment of the bullet's impact upon his back.[9] In the film itself, less than a third of a second after Connally says he was hit, one can see the dramatic effect of the bullet's impact. Between frames 237 and 238, the bullet strike is evident as the Governor's right shoulder collapses, his cheeks suddenly puff, and his hair is disarranged. Indeed, between the two frames, the slope of the Governor's right shoulder suddenly drops by about twenty degrees.[10]

Critics have maintained that because the obvious wounding of the Governor at frames 237-238 occurs only a second and a half after the President could have first been struck by Oswald's rifle it precludes the possibility of a single gunman. I disagree. The critics join the Warren Commission in basing their conclusions on the belief that President Kennedy is reacting, in frames beginning with 225, to a bullet wound. It is more likely, however, that Kennedy is reacting instead to a bullet miss.

Typical of the rush to judgment on the part of the critics is Josiah Thompson, who states in *Six Seconds in Dallas* that "at frame 230 Kennedy has obviously been hit; his hands and elbows are raised; he grimaces." It is hard for me not to grimace as I read Thompson's words. So eager is he to find gunmen in the bushes that he is unwilling to even consider that the President's evident reaction in the film could mean something other than a bullet strike.*

This lack of forethought extends even to more knowledgeable researchers like Dr. John Lattimer, author of *Kennedy and Lincoln*. Dr. Lattimer must subscribe to a "delayed reaction" by Connally because he, too, sees what can't be seen in the Zapruder film—that the President has been wounded by frame 230. In his book, Lattimer abscribes Connally's reactions to something more medically plausible:

> *". . . as his dazed condition wore off a bit, the Governor undoubtedly attempted to take his first breath, with his chest torn open, his fifth rib shattered, his right lung collapsed and cut across the middle lobe. His mouth can be seen to open (in frame 236) and his face contort, reflecting his terrible pain and the frightening sensation of trying to suck air into a damaged lung . . .*[12]

The problem Dr. Lattimer, the Warren Commission and HSCA investigators share is the sudden drop of Connally's right shoulder at frames 237-238. Portions of the human frame don't suddenly drop 20 degrees without some significant outside force acting upon them. And, when you consider that this shoulder drop took place within an eighteenth of a second, that outside force must have been very signifi-

---

* Josiah Thompson believes Connally was shot from the roof of the Dallas County Records Building. Thompson cites the steep angle of the bullet through Connally's body, but ignores the fact that the Governor was obviously leaning backward when he was struck. [13]

cant indeed. Impact on the Governor's back, then, most likely took place at Zapruder frame 237. Interestingly enough, Connally's doctors also reviewed the Zapruder film and placed the moment of impact at about frame 236.[14]

This raises one of the most crucial questions of the continuing assassination controversy. Did the same bullet cause the President's throat wound and all of Governor Connally's wounds as well? Even with the President responding to a bullet hit (as opposed to a miss) at frame 210, if the two men were not hit by the same bullet, there had to be at least two gunmen.

It's important to remember that there's virtually no doubt that all of Connally's bullet wounds were caused by a single missile. All three of the Governor's surgeons agreed on that point. Later, their consensus was confirmed by neutron activation analysis. So, the question becomes this: Did the bullet found on a stretcher at Parkland Hospital cause the President's throat injury and all the Governor's wounds?

It is vital to the critics' case to prove that this single bullet, Commission Exhibit 399, wasn't capable of producing so many injuries. Despite the fact that a bullet can easily pass through two humans, the critics point to the relatively undeformed condition of 399 as proof that it could not have done all the Commission and the HSCA said it did. Indeed, the naysayers have taken to calling the stretcher bullet by another name, the "pristine bullet."*

Commission Exhibit 399 is not pristine. If you don't believe me, go to the National Archives and pick it up for yourself. The critics never bother to point out that the bullet recovered at Parkland is extremely flattened at one end. There's a fair bit of lead core punched out and missing from the bottom of the bullet.

The critics also fail to mention the extremely high muzzle velocity of Oswald's Carcano. A bullet from Oswald's rifle would have overtaken the Presidential limousine at a speed of about 1300 miles per hour. That figure translates just over 2000 feet per second. And, as I mentioned earlier in this book, we have never used carbines of that strength in the United States Army.

---

*I fought long and hard to have photos of the bullet labeled something other than "pristine" in the Sixth Floor exhibit, but to no avail.

This lack of information is a deliberate omission on the part of the critics. Josiah Thompson is the only author I've read who even makes note of the muzzle velocity of the Carcano,[15] but he mentions it in terms of miles per hour, which is irrelevant unless one has a calculator handy.*

The bullet would have lost very little velocity in penetrating President Kennedy's back and throat, since it apparently hit no bone. Since the slits in the President's shirt collar were vertical, I'm led to believe that the bullet was turning nose-down as it left the President's neck. The elongated wound on the Governor's back means that the bullet that struck him entered sideways or at an extreme angle. The possibility of a tangential strike is one that the Warren Commission admitted to,[16] but in this case it's rather unlikely since the bullet continued to follow a straight-line flight path despite the sideways entry.

Bullets don't begin to tumble in mid-air without hitting something first. Since the assassin's view of the Presidential limousine was no longer blocked by the oak tree it is unlikely that a bullet fired from Oswald's rifle at frame 236 of the Zapruder film could have hit anything other than the President before it struck Governor Connally. Furthermore, if Governor Connally had been struck by a bullet from Oswald's rifle which had not hit something first, he would have suffered much greater injury and probably would not be alive today.

Commission Exhibit 399 inflicted the President's throat wound and Governor Connally's wounds and still emerged intact largely because it was turned sideways at the moment of impact with Connally's rib, and flying nearly backwards when it hit the Governor's wrist. Keep in mind that 399 is very flattened at the base end. It's hard to flatten a bullet of this type manually, even by squeezing it in a bench vise. Striking the Governor's fifth rib while flying sideways, though, may well have flattened the bullet to the shape it bears today.

Secondly, the only lead missing from 399 is something on the order of two grains of metal. It's missing from the bottom of the bullet, where the soft lead core has been squeezed out of the base by the flattening action. The metal in the Governor's wrist and the fragment embedded

---

* William Manchester and Jim Bishop both mention the feet-per-second figure, but their books aren't counted among critical literature because they agree with the Report.

in his thigh came from this portion of the bullet.* Despite the critics' hue and cry to the contrary, all of the metal left in Connally could easily be accounted for by the two grains missing from 399.

Assistant Counsel Arlen Specter asked Dr. Charles Gregory, who performed the surgery on the Governor's wrist, to estimate the weight of the fragments of metal left in the wound. Dr. Gregory replied that:

> "I would estimate that they would be weighed in micrograins which is (a) very small amount of weight . . . It is the kind of weighing that requires a microadjustable scale which means that it is something less than the weight of a postage stamp."[17]

Commission Exhibit 399, then, had the potential and capability to hit both Kennedy and Connally and emerge relatively intact. But what about the trajectory? Were Kennedy and Connally aligned so as to produce the wounds the Governor suffered?

The answer is both yes and no. If you mean aligned during the time when the Warren Commission and the HSCA claim Kennedy was first wounded, the answer is probably not. But the two men were in precise alignment during the tenth of a second in which Connally appears to be hit on the Zapruder film.

The HSCA labored long and hard to prove that Kennedy and Connally were in alignment during the interval from film frames 191 to 197.[18] To do so, they used the black-and-white still taken by amateur photographer Hugh Betzner. The problem with the Betzner photo for the Committee's purpose, is that Governor Connally is not visible at all. The HSCA, therefore, used the photo to determine where Governor Connally might have been, since his right shoulder isn't seen in the photograph. This sounds confusing, because it is. The HSCA was trying to place Governor Connally far enough to the left for him to receive a bullet in the back—a bullet that had already passed through Kennedy's neck. From the other side of Elm Street, there's the Zapruder film, which does indeed show Kennedy near the edge of the limousine door and Connally sitting somewhat leftward in front of the President.

---

* Neutron Activation Analysis has proven that the metal recovered from Connally's wrist came from bullet 399. The critics have responded by questioning the chain of possession of the metal fragments. The implication is that someone switched fragments to ensure "favorable" NAA test results. Again, when you give the critics an answer, they either ask another question or make another supposition.

Here a problem emerges. Connally's doctors agreed that the Governor had turned his body to the right by the time he was shot. So, the Governor couldn't have been sitting in front of the President facing straight ahead. In the HSCA diagrams, he isn't. In the Zapruder film, however, he is facing directly ahead of him. Frame 193 of the Zapruder film, for instance shows the Governor's head turned to the right, as he had just heard the sound of a gunshot. His torso is, however, facing forward, and his shirt front and tie are clearly visible in the Zapruder film.

Remember that the HSCA had to gerrymander the Zapruder movie to fit the acoustical evidence, and they obviously took great pains to interpret this crucial photographic evidence in a way that would suit their cause, but in a way contrary to facts deduced by careful study of the film. The photographic expert wasn't asked if the alignment of Kennedy and Connally at frame 197 would produce the Governor's wounds at the angle at which they were inflicted. Medical science was probably not his province, nor is it mine. Nonetheless, the answer is obvious. The Governor's body had to be turned to his right, which doesn't happen until at least frame 234 of the Zapruder film.

The Warren Commission had the same problem in dealing with Zapruder frames 210 through 225. The Governor is sitting somewhat to the President's left, but he is facing forward until he begins to turn to the right after frame 230. So, if indeed Connally was hit by the same bullet which passed through the President's neck, the strike could have occurred no later than frame 240 (according to the Governor's doctors) and no earlier than frame 234 (again, according to the doctors and my own studies) because the two men were not in alignment at any other point. Couple the question of alignment with Connally's obvious reaction visible in the Zapruder film, and there can be little doubt that a shot fired at about Zapruder frame 235 hit the President in the right shoulder, exited his throat, and struck Governor Connally in the back.

Critics who maintain that the two men were hit by separate bullets are faced with a most difficult question: Where did the other bullet go? How could a bullet strike Kennedy in the back, exit his throat, and then just disappear? Since nothing else in the Presidential limousine was struck by a bullet moving at almost full velocity, except for Governor

Connally, it's logical to assume that one bullet did hit both men.*

Obviously, the nature of Governor Connally's wounds and the mute but powerful evidence of the Zapruder film prove that neither the Warren Commission nor the House Select Committee succeeded in providing us with the final answer to the assassination riddle. The Warren Commission, it should be clear, never really conducted an investigation. They began with a conclusion and then worked fairly carefully to ensure that the available facts fit that pre-ordained determination. In a word, they bent their hypothesis to fit the evidence.

The House Select Committee, on the other hand, began with a fairly clean slate and no agenda to pursue. It is unfortunate that, with so much fine work having been done, the HSCA was misled by Chief Counsel Blakey. The end result was that the panel bent the evidence to fit its hypothesis. Nowhere is this more clearly illustrated than the HSCA's treatment of the single-bullet theory and the wounds suffered by Governor Connally.

The theory has been advanced that Oswald, if he did indeed shoot the President, was actually aiming at Governor Connally instead. This is the latest reasoning in an ever widening circle of speculation about Oswald's motive: Since the assassination was too monumental an act to have been committed by a single man, it must have been some sort of conspiracy or a freak accident. Since the facts tend to preclude conspiracies of any sort, the unfortunate accident theory has gained widespread acceptance.

But there's a problem with any theory that postulates Oswald aiming for Connally and hitting Kennedy by mistake. Oswald may well have had a motive for killing Connally. The governor was Secretary of the Navy at the time Oswald fled the Marine Corps and defected to the Soviet Union, receiving a dishonorable discharge in the process. But, Oswald's killing the President was certainly no accident. By the time of the fatal head shot, the Governor had fallen into his wife's arms. He was no longer in line with the President, and Oswald would have had to

---

* This difficulty has led many critics—Josiah Thompson is a case in point—to postulate a bullet shallowly penetrating the President's back, and either a bone fragment or a shot from the front causing the throat wound. With the fairly ready availability of the autopsy photos and x-rays, these speculations have generally been rendered null and void. But there are critics (like Robert Groden) who still propound them, proof still that the critics are relying on the ignorance of the American public to allow them to carry on their misguided efforts.

make a special effort to shoot Connally. As we shall see, he nearly missed hitting the President in the head. Had he really been gunning for the Governor, both men might have survived the attack.

---

1. *New York Times,* November 28, 1963, Edition.
2. *4 Hearings,* 132.
3. Ibid., 135.
4. Ibid., 136.
5. Ibid.
6. WCR, 100.
7. *4 Hearings,* 144.
8. WCR, 109.
9. Thompson, 87.
10. Ibid., 95.
11. Ibid., 87.
12. Lattimer, 261-263.
13. Thompson, 87.
14. Ibid., 174.
I5. Ibid., 83.
16. WCR, 106.
17. Belin, 318.
18. HSCA, II, 185.

XI

The President's Head Wounds

IN PUTTING TOGETHER THE SIXTH FLOOR EXHIBIT, one of the main concerns of the Board of Directors was a tasteful display of photos and motion pictures of the actual assassination. Their decision to avoid a presentation of the head-shot sequence of the Zapruder film, strangely enough, has drawn more criticism from visitors than any other consideration.

Morbid curiosity seekers will always be with us. No matter how refined one might believe the human race to be, there are always those who glory in reliving moments of utter terror and violence. The head-shot sequence is undoubtedly one of these.

Various writers have described Oswald's 88-yard final shot in differing ways. William Manchester, for example, had President Kennedy reaching back to brush back his hair when he was struck by the fatal bullet. We know from the Zapruder film that such a movement never occurred. A better and certainly more accurate description was given by the late Jim Bishop, in his book, *The Day Kennedy Was Shot*:

> The great head was slumping slowly to the left. It came up in the rifle sights big and steady. As before, the rifle jumped, the bullet split the air, and the slower sound swelled through the plaza, tumbling in its echoes. Mrs. Kennedy was staring at her husband. The shell entered the right rear of the skull. A large portion of the head left the body in two chunks. One flew backward into the street. The other fell beside the President. Dura matter, like wet rice, sprayed out of the brain in a pink fan.[1]

Of all the aspects of the assassination seized upon by the critics, the head-shot has been the most sensationalized. These literary ghouls have belabored everything about the President's moment of demise from the grisly autopsy photos to the movement of his shattered skull in the Zapruder film. Why? Because the critics, like circus performers, are aware that the public pays attention to the more morbid aspects of this case. Thus, they focus on them.

Most inexcusable has been the publication by David Lifton (and more recently, Robert Groden) of actual autopsy photos. Were I the dead President's surviving brother, or his son, I would certainly have a difficult time reconciling the public's need to know with my personal sense of dignity and privacy. But such considerations seldom stop the critics. I choose to honor ethics, taste and the dignity of the President.

Perhaps no other chapter in this book will more clearly differentiate me from the tasteless mob. I will not feed on the bloody frenzy they have so successfully generated. I feel less than comfortable, as a historian, with discussing the comments and criticisms of the autopsy photos and x-rays without publishing them. But I will do so, nonetheless. If you're anxious to prove or disprove what I've written, you can go and contribute to Lifton and Groden and cast your vote in favor of their blatant sensationalism.

I mentioned earlier that Lifton's entire book, *Best Evidence,* is based on a chance statement made by a pair of FBI agents after first viewing the President's head wound. His body alteration thesis is a last ditch effort to find some basis of support for the arguments that more than one assassin shot at President Kennedy. If you've read the book, you'll know that Lifton's theory is as ludicrous as it sounds.

Groden on the other hand, adopted a different approach. Since nothing in the autopsy photos and x-rays indicated even one shot from the front, and Groden has been claiming for years that there were several, he charges that the autopsy material has been retouched, painted over, and grossly misrepresented.

The problem, in both cases, is that neither Lifton nor Groden are qualified to read and interpret x-rays and autopsy photos.* I will be first to tell you that I don't either. So, I did what the clear-thinking historian would do in this kind of situation. I asked those who were qualified to interpret what they had seen to do so.

Dr. John Lattimer admittedly carries a pro-Warren Commission

---

* *Neither do some respected critics. When Dr. Cyril Wecht told his briefers what he had seen after his examination of the autopsy materials, one of them responded that Wecht "couldn't even read x-rays."*[2]

bias. But, he is a physician, and has spent years mastering the art of interpreting x-rays. When Groden claimed that in x-rays of the President's head, the right eye socket was missing (the right eye is intact in the autopsy photos), I wrote to Lattimer. Since he had viewed the material, I wanted to know if there was any truth in Groden's charge that someone had altered the autopsy photos. Lattimer replied in a hand-written letter:

> "That line of breakage is well above the eye socket and face. It is where the 'frontal' bone attaches to the upper part of the skull, as it develops.
>
> "X-rays penetrate through and through, making relationships hard to visualize. Thus, there is no discrepancy . . . there was no loss of bone from the face."[3]

Obviously, this is work Groden should have done before he ever sat down at a typewriter. That he didn't do it can be attributed to one of three reasons:

1. *Groden believed he possessed the necessary education and experience to read x-rays; as far as I know he has never been to medical school,*

2. *Groden simply didn't for whatever reasons do the research and assumed the book could stand on its own merits without the effort on his part,*

3. *Groden already knew that professional analysis would disprove his outlandish theories, and thus failed to seek an outside opinion.*

For which explanation would you opt? But remember, we're not playing "Let's Make A Deal," or at least, I'm not. We're adding to the historical record, and what we do should be responsible and carefully documented. Obviously, those constraints hold little weight with Groden.

The bullet wound in the back of President Kennedy's head was fairly high on the rear of the skull where the bone is beginning to curve forward. Thus, the entry wound was oval-shaped, not round. Since the President's head was tilted downward at the time of impact, it might be argued that the bullet skidded along the skull a short distance before entering the cranial vault.[4]

The location of the entry wound makes two things evident. First, Oswald came within an inch or so of missing the President altogether. Second, the autopsy doctors erred by placing the wound much lower in their face sheet and autopsy diagrams. This is probably a justifiable error because they were not allowed to see the x-rays and photographs of the President's body after they had performed the autopsy, and thus had to rely on rough notes and drawings made during the procedure.

The wound of exit covered the front half of the right side of the head, with substantial portions of the top and right half of the scalp and skull missing.[5] This brings us to another popular claim advanced by the critics—that someone is playing fast and loose with the autopsy materials because the doctors at Parkland Hospital recall seeing the head wound at the rear of the skull. Again the explanation for this discrepancy is so simple few will subscribe to it. The Parkland doctors all saw President Kennedy in only one position—face up. An exit wound across his forehead might have been labeled "at the front of the skull," but a wound on the right side? Doctors would have seen the missing area "at the rear of the skull," of course.

In an effort to create a mystery where none existed and to further sensationalize the head wound, Groden and co-author Harrison Livingstone took grainy autopsy photos* to Parkland Hospital and showed them to a few of the doctors who had attended the President back in 1963. Several of the physicians said the wound depicted in the photos bore little resemblance to the one they helped treat on November 22.

The implication was clear. Since Groden rejects Lifton's body-alteration hypothesis, an unusual attitude for Groden, to be sure, the only alternative was that someone had altered the autopsy photos and x-rays to obscure the real nature of the wounds.

This thesis is patently absurd for three important reasons. First, the doctors at Parkland had doubtless treated hundreds upon hundreds of patients since November 22, 1963. Additionally, they had read account after account of the President's wounds, information that wasn't always accurate. So, it's doubtful that any physician would remember the President's wounds in detail. Yet, this was precisely what Groden and Livingstone were basing their theory upon. The fact that the interviews with the doctors took place about twenty years after the fact didn't seem to bother the authors at all.

---

* *Groden was a consultant to the HSCA's photographic panel. One real question is how Groden got copies of the autopsy photos?*

Second, the autopsy surgeons themselves authenticated the x-rays and photographs taken of the dead President's body. Since Groden knew this, he and Livingston probably realized that their only opportunity to stir up controversy was to go to Parkland and talk with the doctors there.

Finally, the Zapruder film shows the President's head wound in exactly the position the autopsy photos and x-rays depict it. Groden postulates an additional wound at the lower rear of the head which would have been invisible to the Parkland doctors because, you'll recall, the President was never turned over. Minor details such as this, however, don't seem to bother Groden.

Groden, Lifton, and the other critics make much of the fact that Kennedy's brain, which was removed and not buried with him, is missing from the National Archives. The brain would offer little or nothing in the way of new evidence, since it was photographed and x-rayed prior to and immediately following removal.[6] Yet, the critics claim that it's missing from the National Archives because it would prove their contention that another gunman was firing at the President. Just how the brain would yield this new information is never really discussed. The House Select Committee probed deeply into the case of the missing brain. They concluded that Robert Kennedy, for reasons of privacy or to avoid future public display, destroyed or buried the steel cannister containing the brain.

I should stress again that all medical evidence in this case points to a single bullet, fired from behind, entering the right rear high of the President's head. The bullet's entry is fairly well established because bone at the rear of the skull is pushed inward around the point of impact. Continuing through the brain, the missile obviously exited the right side of the President's skull, causing a massive fracture. Continuing across the body of the Presidential limousine, the bullet apparently struck the inside of the windshield glass, broke into two pieces, and dropped to the floor. The fragments were recovered there late on the night of the assassination. Neutron activation analysis proved that a fragment lodged near the President's right eye matched the fragments recovered from the limousine floor.[7]

The critics, however, have had a field day contending otherwise.

Since the Zapruder film clearly shows Kennedy thrown back against the car seat by the impact of the fatal shot, the naysayers invoke the aid of a Newtonian law of physics that leads them to believe that the shot came from the right front and, as a result, drove the President backward and to his left. There's no medical evidence to support this contention, just as there's no hard physical evidence to give credence to the second gunman theory. But since so much of the critics' success is based on their examination of the movement of Kennedy's body, this is a hard contention for us to ignore.

Josiah Thompson, for example, devoted nearly fifty pages of *Six Seconds in Dallas* to careful photographic measurements and eyewitness testimony which led him to believe that the President had in fact been hit twice: first from the rear, and then from the front. This double-impact was the result, Thompson said, of two rifle shots fired almost simultaneously.[8]

On its surface, the evidence Thompson presents is somewhat compelling. In 1967, when his book was first published, there was no access to the autopsy photos and x-rays which would have settled the question. Today, with that evidence available, Dr. Thompson's theory faces additional problems.

First, there's nothing in the medical evidence to suggest a shot from the right front. Even Dr. Cyril Wecht admits that the possibility of a shot from the knoll having struck the President in the head is highly unlikely. Wecht, who disagreed with the HSCA medical evidence panel at almost every point, was questioned about the possibility of a head-shot from the front, and admitted that there was no supporting evidence: "Yes, with reasonable medical certainty I would have to say that the evidence is not there. I have already said it is a remote possibility and I certainly cannot equate that with reasonable medical certainty."[9]

The fact "that the evidence is not there" has failed to impede the efforts of critics like Groden, Lifton, and former New Orleans District Attorney Jim Garrison from bringing forth the old suppositions of a gunman on the knoll.

It's also helpful to understand that the movement of the President's head as seen in the Zapruder film isn't immediately backward. Indeed, his head moves forward slightly as a result of the impact of the bullet on the back of the skull. Only after the bullet has obviously torn through his brain and blown out the right side of his head does Kennedy begin the rapid and forceful movement backward.

For all the critics' turgid writings about the backwards head-snap, the House Select Committee's medical evidence panel put the question to rest in a single paragraph:

> "The majority of the panel believes that there is a possibility that this movement may have been caused by neurologic response to the massive brain damage caused by the bullet, or by a propulsive effect resulting from the matter that exited through the large defect under great pressure, or a combination of both."[10]

This jet effect theory has its adherents, this author being one of them. In 1975, *Time* magazine's Ed Magnuson wrote that Dr. Lattimer and others had conducted experiments that yielded some amazing results that bore directly on the question of the head snap. Magnuson noted that :

> "Lattimer, again, has done grisly but practical experiments on Kennedy's head movements. As do other analysts, he notes that the head momentarily moves forward in one frame of the film before jolting more noticeably backward, Lattimer and his sons have fired the Oswald-type gun and ammunition into the rear of human skulls packed with gelatin. He has films to show that in each case the skulls toppled backward off their stands, never forward. Similar tests were conducted with melons by Physicist Luis Alvarez of the University of California, with the same results. Though neither had expected this movement, they theorized that the escape of material through the larger exit wounds in these tests had a jet-like effect that propelled the melons and skulls to the rear."[11]

Little I've said in this chapter will sway the die-hard scoffers. They'll continue to believe in shots from the grassy knoll, despite the lack of evidence to support their view. They will continue to assert that autopsy photos and x-rays have been switched or altered, despite their lack of proof and ample evidence to the contrary.

Why, then, do so many people believe that President Kennedy moved backward in response to a shot from the front? Or that his missing brain holds the key to the assassination controversy? The answer is simple—because they want to. Some people rely on their feelings, while others tend to look for something more substantial in which to place their trust. In this case, the evidence is real, substantial, and reasonable, unlike the arguments advanced by the critics.

The problem with the evidence is that it forces us to some pretty obvious conclusions. Eventually, regardless of our convictions, it makes us realize that the crime which robbed us of our President happened as we were told it did, with a few minor exceptions. Those exceptions are reconciled with the evidence in the chapter that follows.

1. Bishop, 152.
2. Lattimer, letter to the author December 1, 1989.
3. Weisberg, *Post Mortem*, (Fredrick, Maryland: self-published 1975), 626.
4. Lattimer, *Kennedy and Lincoln*, 211.
5. Ibid., 210.
6. Ibid., 197.
7. Ibid., 217.
8. Thompson, 105-151.
9. HSCA, VII, 178.
10. Ibid.
11. *Time*, November 24, 1975, 37.

XII

The Final Solution

FOR THREE HEADLINE DAYS IN THE SPRING OF 1990, Cleburne Texas attorney Gary Shaw—founder of the "JFK Assassination Research Center" that competes for tourist dollars with the Sixth Floor exhibit—bragged that he and Texas-based investigator Jim West had solved the Kennedy assassination.

Radio station KLIF in Dallas (normally a paragon of sobriety and reason) apparently believed Shaw wholesale without demanding to see the proof of the plot. Accordingly, popular morning-show host Kevin McCarthy invited Shaw and West to appear on his program via a long-distance telephone hook-up.

The results were predictable. Shaw, promising that the information would be forthcoming, refused to name names or produce evidence. Under close questioning by call-in listeners, he did admit that the two "assassins" he and West had "found" just happened to be deceased.

Shaw stepped into quicksand when he mentioned that his source of information was a now carefully guarded former prison inmate. The two actual murderers had, in turn, confessed their crime to this man. Again, both had subsequently died. The fact that Shaw was relying on an ex-con as his only information source seemed not to bother him at all.

I listened to the show via a special radio hookup in my office in Waco. I must admit that some points of the program induced laughter, especially when Shaw claimed to have proof that Lee Harvey Oswald had committed no crime on November 22, 1963. Within five minutes, assassination researcher Carl Henry called in to inform Shaw, West, and host McCarthy that he had an eyewitness to the Tippit killing (previously undiscovered by official investigators) who positively identified

Oswald as the murderer. Apparently, the witness had been laying tile in a neighborhood house, watched the shooting, and stared in blank amazement as Oswald trotted away, heading along the sidewalk directly in front of the home.

Predictably, Shaw evidenced no interest in Henry's novel and stunning disclosure. Host McCarthy, irked that someone armed with factual information might dare to throw cold water on his already-foundering program, cut Henry off. McCarthy never managed to acquit himself of this fiasco, despite stating on-air several times that Shaw had promised to name names and produce evidence and then had welched on his commitment. McCarthy twice stated his belief that the photos and x-rays of the President's body had been altered, citing as proof of this absurd allegation the "facts" presented by critic Robert Groden in *High Treason*.

You readers know by now that, in my opinion, *High Treason* is a compendium of heresay and misinformation. When the program was over and my laughter had subsided, I dictated a letter to McCarthy in which I sought to present the truth about the events surrounding the assassination. Claiming the usual station-tendered offer of equal time, I wrote McCarthy's producer, Connie Herrera, that "thirty minutes on-air is all I need to demolish your fabricated case." I mentioned McCarthy's misplaced endorsement of Groden's book, and added: "Kevin either needs to read a lot more about the assassination or stop reading altogether." I ended by declaring my willingness, in any forum, to debate Shaw and West and added my firm belief that the truth in the case—that Oswald was the lone assassin—would prevail.

My letter went unanswered. I was reminded of David Belin's letters to Mark Lane, in which the former Warren Commission Assistant Counsel sought to accept Lane's offer to appear in Lane's *Rush to Judgment* companion film. You'll remember that Belin, in his final letter, chided Lane for his failure to make good on his original offer, then added: "The reason is obvious—you were afraid ... afraid of the truth." Since the truth doesn't appear to sell radio programs, I submit that Kevin McCarthy and KLIF are afraid as well.

Gary Shaw knows that if the lurid displays in his Dallas "Research Center" were to proclaim the truth that Oswald was the lone assassin, he would have no business from the tourist traffic. Had David Lifton's *Best Evidence* video tape presentation contained the truth, it would not have sold faster than book store employees could put it on the shelves. Had Fort Worth journalist Jim Marrs been interested in the truth, his best-seller *Crossfire* would never have been written.

I believe that you readers, and the American public, are interested in the truth. But the assassination sensationalists have done so fine a job packaging speculation and rumor that we must at least credit their industry. Unfortunately, their priorities are somewhat misplaced. Adding to the historical record and promoting a solution to the crime of the century should come before personal gain and headlong limelight. And so this final solution is born. To be sure, it will not answer all the questions—just the most important ones.

When friends ask me about the assassination, they usually focus on a pair of questions: (1) *Did Oswald really do it?* (2) *What was his motive?* Both will be answered forthwith.

Throughout this book, Lee Harvey Oswald has been flatly referred to as the assassin of President Kennedy and Officer Tippit. No qualifiers such as "alleged" or "presumed" have been used. The mark of guilt is as plainly upon him as it was upon banished Cain.

But through the decades, responsible historians have been faced with the almost overwhelming task—of reconciling the evidence that proclaims Oswald's guilt with the eyewitness testimony and the critics' supposition. That is the purpose of this chapter, since that somber reckoning has fallen to me.

Dr. Michael Baden chaired the House Select Committee's forensics panel. In his book, *Unnatural Death*, Dr. Baden describes how the group was nearly misled by Counsel Blakey and the assassination sensationalists. Clearly, the evidence developed by Dr. Baden's panel was conclusive: all the shots which hit President Kennedy and Governor Connally were fired from behind and somewhat to the right. There were no shots from the right front. The HSCA, building on the forensics panel's work, determined that the bullets which struck the two men were fired from Oswald's rifle. The identity of the assassin who had fired the fatal shots had been determined with finality.

But the critics refused to accept their own demise. Even today, they contend that this case is strangely without a "smoking gun." With ease they apparently discount the eyewitness testimony of Howard Brennen, who saw Oswald in the sixth-floor window and stood helpless as the assassin took aim for the final, fatal shot. They discount the mysterious paper bag, found alongside the sniper's window, despite the fact that the bag bore Oswald's palm print and despite eyewitness testimony that he carried such a bag to work with him on the morning of the assassination. Oswald lied to the police when he told officers that, at the moment of the assassination, he was eating lunch with James Jarman Jr., in the Book Depository's lunchroom on the second floor. Since Jarman was photographed on the fifth floor at the time of the assassination, Oswald apparently lacked even the weakest alibi. And to my knowledge, only one book out of the hundreds of volumes on the assassination has mentioned Oswald's nervous mis-purchase of a Coca-Cola moments after he fired the fatal shot.

So you see, when one discounts the best available eyewitness testimony—and the interrogation of the assassin himself—this case does appear to be strangely without a "smoking gun." But when that evidence, much of which is oddly ignored by the critics and sensationalists, is added to the monumental record, there can be no doubt that Oswald was the assassin (and the sole assassin) of President Kennedy and Officer Tippit.

Confronted with the weight of the hard physical evidence, the critics have been forced to retreat and regroup. Then, led by David Lifton into the 1980s, the professional contrarians have beguiled the American people into the belief that the evidence of a conspiracy was present before the government (or their various, unnamed conspirators-at-large) had the opportunity to alter it. Flatly, books like *Best Evidence* and *High Treason* elevate the science of grasping at straws to new heights.

David Lifton, for his part, claims to be a student of forensics and ballistics. Yet he apparently was either ignorant of or chose to ignore the fact that injuries inflicted on a post-mortem body (a corpse) can be easily distinguished from premortem injuries. If someone had altered the President's body during the trip from Dallas to Bethesda, the autopsy doctors would have been readily able to discern the alterations. You readers can scour the hundreds of pages of Lifton's book for a single mention of rigor mortis, algor mortis and livor mortis. There is none to be found.

Groden's absurd conclusion that a massive wound at the rear of the President's head provided proof of the plot and has been hidden in the autopsy x-rays and photographs simply does not correspond with the available photographic and eyewitness evidence. Not one Dealey Plaza witness saw Kennedy struck in the rear of the head, nor did anyone testify that he saw the lower back of the President's skull erupt. Groden, however, does a good job of gerrymandering the testimony and photographs to fit his conclusion that someone doctored the x-rays. His efforts remind me of a child hammering on a puzzle piece that obviously needs a little coaxing to fit properly.

Groden's book and Lifton's, for that matter, would have been unthinkable as recently as two decades ago. Back then, the first-generation critics were having a field day with what we couldn't see, the x-rays and photographs of the President's body. Mark Lane, in particular, claimed in *Rush to Judgment* that there was no evidence to support an entry wound in the rear of the skull, save for a mark on a crude autopsy face sheet. Lane's implication was obvious: the head shot had come from the front; the rear entry wound had been "invented" by the authorities to shore up the single-assassin theory.

But beginning with the Ramsey Clark panel in the late 1960s, the facts began to assume traction. Years later, the House Select Committee conducted the most indepth study to date; its conclusion pointed to all wounds from one gun behind and above. That would have settled the matter, but for the critics' empty bank accounts. Even at this late date, the President's body remains the object of obscene speculation, and the autopsy photographs and x-rays have become the province of every sewing circle and locker room across the land.

There is no reason for the speculation to remain rampant, except the public's willingness to support the most outlandish critics and to believe virtually anything displayed as evidence. I also fault the critics' willingness to publish literally anything, so long as it is lurid. Dr. Baden, the chairman of the HSCA's forensics panel, tried to put an end to the rumor and innuendo regarding the physical evidence and the President's body:

> *"The variety of conspiracy theories had called into question every bit of evidence, including the body itself. According to one scenario, during the plane ride from Dallas to Washington the entrance wounds were altered to look like exit wounds in order to confuse everyone about the direction of the shots. According to another, the original autopsy report, photographs, and x-rays had all been stolen from the National Archives and replaced with fakes. I wondered at the vast numbers of people that would have been required to carry out all these tasks and the extraordinary combination of luck, competence, and intelligence, so lacking in all other human endeavors, that would have been needed to pull off these delicate and complex conspiracies in secret—and have them remain secret."*[1]

There is little doubt as to the identities of the twin conspiracy theories Baden refers to. They originated in the minds of David Lifton and Robert Groden. Which side do you believe? Well, consider for a moment that neither Groden nor Lifton is a trained forensic pathologist. In fact, neither is a trained investigator. Baden is both. Neither Groden nor Lifton is former Chief Medical Examiner for one of the largest cities in the world. Baden is. And neither critic can rightfully be accused of putting the truth about the assassination at the head of his own personal agenda.

Dr. Baden goes even further toward completely discrediting the critics. In a single line, he delivers the coup de grace to assassination sensationalists like Marrs, Thompson and Lane who still subscribe to phantom gunmen atop the grassy knoll: "There was NO EVIDENCE that anything had hit the President from the front."[2] The emphasis is mine. The quote stands alone as a model of clarity.

When the critics swing their sights to the single-bullet theory, Dr. Baden is even more emphatic. Here, Baden has done something few, if any, critics have ever done—he has personally examined the scars borne by the other gentleman wounded that day in Dealey Plaza. During the course of the HSCA investigation, Baden met with Governor Connally and asked the Texan to remove his jacket and shirt. The Governor complied, and as Baden related: "There it was—a two-inch long sideways entrance scar in his back. He had not been shot by a second shooter but by the same flattened bullet that went through

Kennedy."[3]

The previous three chapters, have detailed descriptions of the wounds suffered by both the President and the Governor. Much of what you've read has been based on my own impressions, which have, in turn, been based on years of research. I've included Dr. Baden's comments here to illustrate to even the die-hard skeptics that those most familiar with the case (and without an axe of their own to grind at the public expense) believe that a lone assassin wounded Governor Connally and killed President Kennedy. On the basis of the evidence detailed in this book, there can be no doubt that the lone assassin was Lee Harvey Oswald. He committed the crime of the century, acting totally alone.

Any number of interesting cases can be made for the sequence of the three shots Oswald fired; reading books and watching dozens of television programs on the assassination, I have studied some which were actually humorous. In his fine book, *The Assassination of President Kennedy — The Reasons Why*, author Albert Newman delivers sound theory regarding the assassin's motive.* Still, Newman obviously felt compelled to devote several pages to the notion that Oswald fired a final shot after the bullet which shattered Kennedy's skull.

When one sits in the reconstructed sixth-floor window and surveys Elm Street below, Newman's assertion becomes somewhat ludicrous. Oswald must have seen Kennedy's head explode at Zapruder-frame 313; to suggest that his eye would have been trained on something else besides his quarry fixed in the Carcano's telescopic sight is foolhardy, given the fact that he had just fired the fatal shot a tenth of a second earlier. Newman suggests that Oswald hit the President in the back of the skull with his second shot, and that, preparing for his third, he deliberately threw his aim for fear of hitting Mrs. Kennedy as she climbed onto the car trunk. Newman wrote:

> *"And so it may be that while Clinton Hill (the Secret Service agent who climbed aboard the limousine and pushed Mrs. Kennedy back into the rear*

---

* *Newman believes that Oswald had help in carrying out his unsuccessful April 1963 attempt on the life of right-wing activist General Edwin Walker, and that the assassin, after shooting the President, retrieved his pistol from his rooming house with the intention of gunning down the General in a final act of defiant violence on November 22.*[4]

seat) saved Jacqueline Kennedy from death or serious injury under the wheels of the tailgating Secret Service car by pushing her into her seat . . . the First Lady saved the Secret Service agent from similar perils by gunshot through her presence behind him in Oswald's sight. With Oswald's probable reaction in mind, I deem it quite possible that the last bullet of the series that killed the President of the United States lies somewhere in the mud grasses of the Trinity River flats in the direction of Oak Cliff." [5]

Had more people bought Newman's book when it was published in 1979, there might have been legions of treasure hunters armed with metal detectors swarming over the Trinity River banks in search of Oswald's final bullet. The fact that there wasn't one there would probably not have deterred them.

The longer it took Oswald to reach the second-floor lunchroom, the more likely that an officer would stop him en route. Why then would he continue to risk detection, returning fire by Secret Service agents, and police capture, to fire a final shot at a target who had already been obviously mortally wounded?

The answer is that he wouldn't. But the problem author Newman faced in 1970 is the problem already solved in this book. He had no way to determine precisely the timing of the first shot, even though the tools for that determination lay at his fingertips. In any case, he certainly had access to the Zapruder film, which clearly shows the Governor responding to bullet wounds a half-second after the President shows a reaction to some external stimuli.

It took me ten years to determine the precise timing of the first shot fired at President Kennedy. I spent another four years making sure I was right. What Newman overlooked were, in effect, pieces of the puzzle that seemed unrelated. I do not fault Newman for giving those pieces little weight.

Jim Bishop, in *The Day Kennedy Was Shot*, places too much significance on the Zapruder film when he notes that: "The best procedure is to work backwards. Zapruder's film proves that the third shot blew the top off of John Kennedy's head." [6] The Zapruder film may contain many things, but it does not include sound. Bishop's independent determination had no basis in fact. To give credit to Albert Newman, there is no way anyone can determine, from photographic or physical evidence, which shots hit and which one missed.*

William Manchester tried to skirt the issue of the missed shot by ignoring it altogether. His dramatic and inaccurate reconstruction of the assassination omits mention of a shot that did not hit. Indeed, in *The Death of a President*, the author makes the point that: " . . . it would have been typical of Oswald's laxity to have come to the warehouse with an expended cartridge in the breech, which would have required removal before he could commence firing."[7] In a word, Manchester advocated the avoidance of a mystery by choosing to believe that Oswald fired only two shots when the vast majority of eyewitnesses heard three.

The Warren Commission, of course, considered each of the three shots in an effort to determine which was the most likely to have missed the President and the Governor. Each had its merits on this point. The commission wrote that the first shot may have been poorly aimed:

"If the first shot missed, the assassin perhaps missed in an effort to fire a hurried shot before the President passed under the oak tree, or possibly he fired as the President passed under the tree and the tree obstructed his view. The bullet might have struck a portion of the tree and been completely deflected."[8]

The Report clearly indicated a leaning by its authors toward a second-shot miss:

"The possibility that the second shot missed is consistent with the elapsed time between the two shots that hit their mark. From the timing evidenced by the Zapruder films, [sic] there was an interval of from 4.8 to 5.6 seconds between the shot which struck President Kennedy's neck (between frames 210 and 225) and the shot which struck his head at frame 313. Since a minimum of 2.3 seconds must elapse between shots, a bullet could have been fired from the rifle and missed during this interval."[9]

Six years before Albert Newman's conjecture, the Commission gave little weight to a third-shot miss, noting that: "one must consider, however, the testimony of the witnesses who described the head shot as the concluding event in the assassination sequence."[10] The Commission noted the difficulty of determining with certainty just which shot

---

* My determination is based on eyewitness testimony, which I generally consider unreliable. In this particular instance, however, the testimony is so unique and reliable as to be considered valid and noteworthy.

failed to find its mark, adding that:

> *"The wide range of possibilities and the existence of conflicting testimony, when coupled with the impossibility of scientific verification, precludes a conclusive finding by the Commission as to which shot missed."* [11]

The Commission's reenactments and ballistics experiments were unremarkable, except for the lack of attention to detail. Years later the House Select Committee would offer up charts, graphs, and drawings based upon fine work in photo enhancement and trajectory analysis. All the Warren Commission really furnished us was a fairly exact position for the Presidential limousine at the time the shots were fired. This was enough, considering the lack of technical refinement in the early and mid-'60s.

The reenactment conducted by the FBI for the Commission used the Zapruder film as a reference. Photos taken from Zapruder's position during the reenactment were compared with the originals. Even to the untrained observer, lack of attention to detail is obvious. The angles of each camera view are grossly different. The phrase, "Close enough for government work" does come to mind.

What the Commission could only conjecture from a ballistics standpoint, the HSCA came close to proving in the late '70s. The single-bullet theory seemed all but a certainty, given the HSCA analysis of the bullet flightpaths through both men. Of course, much of this fine work was obscured when it was willfully gerrymandered by Chief Counsel Blakey and his cohorts in their attempt to prove that the assassination was more than a "conspiracy" of one.

But it's wise to bear in mind that the HSCA had something the Warren Commissioners never even saw: the autopsy x-rays and photographs of the body of John Kennedy. And while the Warren Commission's trajectory work could have been accomplished by any high school shop team with a surveyor's transit, the reenactment was probably the best that could be hoped for, given the data available to those who staged it.

In presenting my final solution to the assassination of President Kennedy, then, I am relying on the pure, unadulterated physical evidence, and upon the findings of those qualified to interpret accurately the autopsy photos and x-rays. Additionally, I have gained great insight by spending countless hours at the scene of the crime. I have, as

I mentioned in the preface to this book, agonized over the final solution day and night for years.

In a word, it is as accurate a portrayal as I can humanly make it. Based upon the credible evidence and upon select eyewitness testimony, it is the best possible reconstruction of what really happened in Dealey Plaza on November 22, 1963. To all those who insist otherwise will fall the awesome burden of proving me wrong.

A handful of eyewitnesses hold the key to the assassination riddle. First is Phil Willis, who took the series of slides before, during, and after the assassination. His fifth slide, according to Willis, was taken immediately following the sound of the first shot. You'll remember Willis testifying that the crack of the first explosion caused him to squeeze the camera shutter as a reflex response.

As I pointed out earlier, Willis is visible in the Zapruder film. It's evident that Willis has taken his camera down from his eye by Zapruder frame 204. Three frames later, he disappears from the film forever. Having lowered his camera by frame 204, though, would indicate that Willis had taken slide five some time earlier, most likely before frame 190. Could Willis have been wrong in his testimony? Could he have imagined that he took his slide as a reflex to the sound of the first shot? That's unlikely. I've spent hours talking with Mr. Willis. He's no stranger to tragedy. His reactions have been sharpened by participation in the defense of Pearl Harbor and service with distinction during World War II.

What if Willis had taken his slide by frame 190? What does a single slide prove? Remember the basic Warren Commission re-enactment that showed, except for a brief instant at frame 186, the assassin's view of the motorcade was obscured by the branches of a large oak tree. The Commission, considering it unlikely that Oswald would have fired through the branches, postulated that Kennedy could first have been hit by frame 210 just as he passed behind the road sign that obscures him from Zapruder's camera.

I believe that Oswald did shoot through the break in the foliage. I believe that this first, hurried shot missed. Casual readers might call this unimportant. If the bullet didn't hit anything, why bother? I didn't say it didn't hit anything. I merely said it missed both the President and the

Governor.

The first shot struck the Elm Street roadway near the right rear of the limousine. Bounding low beneath the auto, it ranged diagonally across Dealey Plaza and struck the south Main Street curbway. The impact knocked pieces of concrete into the face of spectator James Tague, who reported the incident to police.

I believe that President Kennedy shared Tague's experience. Doubtless the bullet hitting the concrete only a few feet from the President showered President Kennedy with bits of concrete and possibly metal fragments. Since the bullet struck to the right rear of the limousine, it's likely no one else was affected by the missed shot.

Five eyewitnesses saw either the bullet strike the pavement or its aftermath. The fact that only five witnesses out of hundreds in Dealey Plaza should see this isolated incident testifies to the fact that it actually happened. Everyone else should have been watching the President and the Governor, and not the roadway behind the limousine. Mrs. Virgie Baker was standing on the north curb of Elm Street as the shots were fired. She told Warren Commission counsel Wes Liebeler that she saw something hit the pavement in the middle lane, behind the Presidential automobile. Researchers note that Mrs. Baker did give conflicting versions of her testimony at different times, but her Commission testimony is validated by four other witnesses. Mr. and Mrs. Jack Franzen were standing a few feet down Elm Street from Mrs. Baker. Both noticed small fragments flying about inside the President's car immediately following the first shot. Postal Inspector Harry Holmes saw the bullet strike the roadway through binoculars from his office across the Plaza. And Royce Skelton, atop the triple overpass, saw pieces of concrete fly up at the rear of the limousine.

Oswald, then, missed his first shot, fired at about frame 186, using the Zapruder film as our clock. Perhaps the bullet was deflected at first by a tree branch. The slug struck the concrete behind and to the right side of the Presidential automobile. As far as I can determine, no examination of the road surface was ever undertaken before Elm Street was repaved some months after the assassination.

President Kennedy, of course, heard the sound of the first shot. Pelted or forcibly struck by bits of concrete and metal, he lived the next two seconds in a daze. His right arm, which had been waving to the Elm Street crowd, froze in place. By the time he emerged from behind the road sign and back into Zapruder's view, his hands were rising to cover his face. Critics and investigators alike have universally assumed that as the President reappears in the Zapruder film, he is reacting to a bullet wound. I submit that he is reacting instead to a gunshot, one which missed but was nonetheless felt.

By frame 230 of the Zapruder film, Governor Connally is facing straight ahead as he prepares to turn to his right. Connally has heard the sound of a rifle shot, and is making the turn to see if he could spot the President in the corner of his vision. Nearly two-and-a-half seconds have elapsed since the first shot, long enough for Lee Harvey Oswald to work the Carcano bolt and draw a fresh bead with the Italian rifle.

A third of a second later, Kennedy and Connally are hit. The change in the angle of the Governor's right shoulder, the expansion of his cheeks as his lung collapses, and the musing of his hair all illustrate the impact of the bullet on the Governor. President Kennedy, his hands clenched in front of his face, was struck first by the bullet which went on to wound Connally. Hit in his raised right shoulder, the slug has drilled through soft tissue in Kennedy's neck and emerged next to the knot in his necktie, passing beneath his upraised hands. Almost immediately, the President's hands begin a rapid drop to his throat. By frame 255, a second later his fists are grabbing for his punctured windpipe. Contrary to popular opinion, the President would have faced a difficult recovery from this first wound.

Kennedy has been wounded, *perhaps* not severely. Oswald is at a distinct disadvantage because he cannot see the President's face. He takes his time preparing for his third shot. A fourth cartridge is in the clip, but he may need it in the event a fellow Depository employee is still crouched near a window on the still, sixth floor.

For more than four seconds, the assassin tracks the back of the President's head. As the car continues to coast slowly down the Elm Street slope, he squeezes the trigger. Moving at nearly twice the speed of sound the bullet impacts on the back of Kennedy's head at frame 312 in the Zapruder film. In the next frame, the right side of the President's skull seems to explode.

Blood and brain burst from the disrupted cranial vault as the force of the escaping tissue hurtles the President backward and to his left. His brain is quite destroyed, and Kennedy is literally dead before he hits the car seat. Although his heart will continue to beat during the six-minute journey to Parkland, nothing can be done.

To the best reckoning of physical evidence, eyewitness testimony, and the photographic record, this is a valid reconstruction of the assassination of President Kennedy. It relies on the testimony of six witnesses, counting the Franzens separately. Phil Willis kept his head during Pearl Harbor, and it stands to reason that he'd accurately remember the shock of the first shot causing him to squeeze his camera shutter. Mrs. Baker's testimony is validated by the Franzens, who are in turn supported by Holmes and Skelton.

The timing of the first shot is crucial, since this reconstruction depends on Oswald having enough time to miss with the first shot, then hit with his second. Willis, fortunately, is visible in the Zapruder film, and has obviously taken his slide by frame 204. Working backwards, one can conclude that the shot he responded to was fired roughly a second earlier. The FBI and Secret Service reenactments both show a break in the tree foliage at about frame 186. It seems logical to me to postulate that Oswald seized this opportunity to squeeze off the shot, or that he was nervous and rushed his first opportunity. Both are possibilities. No one will ever know for certain.

Readers may well ask why I have singled out relatively unknown eyewitness testimony while ignoring those whose accounts are better known. The reason is simple. There is very little in the way of eyewitness testimony in this case which can be trusted. A great deal is contradictory, and much makes no sense at all. The photographs and motion pictures taken at the time of the assassination have been both a blessing and a curse to researchers. But they've contributed much over the years toward helping us see that many eyewitnesses testified to things that never really happened at all.

Phil Willis is the only eyewitness to have been present at another major tragedy: the bombing of Pearl Harbor. If anyone in Dealey Plaza that day knew how to think clearly in a time of crisis, Willis did. Governor Connally's recollections have always been consistent, even though they did not agree with the conclusions of official investigators. They happen to coincide perfectly with the final solution I've devised. The Franzens and Mrs. Baker were all in a position to observe the effects of the first missed shot and their testimony is so patently unique that it would have been imprudent to discount it.

The physical evidence is, on the other hand, a model of clarity. Here, all that is to be seen can be seen. The fragments of bullets recovered from the front of the Presidential limousine caused Kennedy's massive head wound. The stretcher bullet recovered at Parkland Hospital did indeed pass through both the President and the Governor, and no matter what the critics say, it is *not* pristine. Both rounds came from Oswald's rifle to the exclusion of all other weapons in the world. One could hardly ask for a stronger tie.

The pre-arranged stacks of book cartons convinced me that the assassination had been carefully planned over a period of several hours. And, despite the inconsistencies in eyewitness testimony regarding the length of the wrapping paper bag, the official explanation for its presence has never really been superseded by another. Oswald obviously used it that morning, but for what? Curtain rods? Not likely. Would he have gone to so much trouble to so carefully wrap curtain rods? Do you really think he carried them to work that day? The critics should quit kidding themselves. Oswald had his rifle in that bag. His palm print is mute evidence that he carried it into the building. No other explanation makes any sense.

I believe that Oswald spent his morning work hours assembling the rifle and the shields of cartons around the corner window. I think he waited patiently until the President swung into view, and fired three shots. My hours in the corner window have convinced me that his task was an easy one. Interestingly enough, virtually every visitor I've escorted to the sniper's nest re-creation has remarked to me their surprise at the apparently easy shot Oswald had.

And now, another question. Why did Oswald shoot the President? Did someone encourage him to murder Kennedy? Or did the idea spring into his mind on the afternoon of November 21, when he learned of the parade route? Did he return to Irving in a last-ditch effort to reconcile with his wife, or because his rifle was there?

Let me state from the first that I do not believe, because of Oswald's psychopathy, that he would ever have allowed anyone to become close enough to him to suggest the assassination. Oswald was too much a loner, and fiercely independent enough to reject any hint or suggestion that might shape his future actions. It's interesting to me that Oswald's family (his mother excepted, of course) has always believed that he killed Kennedy alone, without help.*

If those closest to Oswald, his wife, and brother, believe that he could not have been approached with an entreaty to murder the President, then how did the idea cross Oswald's mind? I believe that it first manifested itself on the afternoon of November 21 when Oswald learned that Kennedy's motorcade would take him down Elm Street in front of the Depository.

Oswald, it must be said, saw himself as an individual of some significance who had been virtually ignored by the stage of history. Notoriety, good or bad, probably meant more to him than anything else on earth. Truthfully, he had failed at life. With a wife and two children he could barely support, existing on a $1.25-an-hour job, having been banned from Cuba despite his intent to help Castro, one might say that the young man had little to live for. Going out in style in a blaze of glory was much more satisfying an alternative than continuing to exist in a purgatory of daily boredom and frustration.

I do not believe that anything Marina said or did influenced Oswald's decision on the night of November 21. Regardless of what the young woman said to her husband, the die had been cast. Oswald went to Irving to say goodbye to his daughter and to pick up his rifle. I find it doubtful that the assassin ever entertained a second thought.

Put yourself in Oswald's place. Thwarted by life at every turn, yoked to an unhappy spouse and saddled with the responsibility for two small children, living hand-to-mouth by virtue of a job unsuited to someone with your mentality, you might have thought, as Oswald did, that fate had been dropped into your lap. And who is to say that any one of us, as desperate as Oswald must have been, would not have seized the opportunity to end our suffering and gain a place in history? Lee

---

* *Marina now says she believes organized crime aided her husband.*

Harvey Oswald may well be the first man in recorded history to have plunged the entire world into mourning simply to become well-known by doing so.

Friends often ask me why I think Oswald shot the president. Most often, they're looking for a motive rather than a detailed review of the physical evidence. My answer is that I believe the assassin was at the end of his mental and emotional rope, and saw Kennedy's visit to Dallas as a vehicle to propel him out of an existence he hated and into the history books.

I believe Oswald expected to be killed when he was arrested at the Texas Theater. You don't pull a pistol on an armed police officer and not expect to be shot in response. Doubtless, the fact that he left the theater alive must have been an incredible surprise to him. Indeed, in trying to understand Oswald, I've come to believe that he felt disdain for being alive throughout the assassination weekend. For him, the end could not have come too quickly. His family members may disagree, but I believe that, until he lost consciousness, Lee saw Jack Ruby's bullet as a most painful blessing, a benediction of sorts at the end of his life.

Oswald probably enjoyed some sort of mental moment of triumph in the seconds after he fired the fatal shot at President Kennedy. Kennedy, to be sure, was everything Oswald was not—rich, handsome, mature, powerful, loved, respected—and Oswald shot him as casually as you and I might shoot at tin cans in an empty lot. Truly, in this moment of desperate horror and incredible loss, Oswald must have felt something akin to a sense of pride because he, a self-centered, pathetic loser by virtually anyone's standard, had just killed the most powerful man in the entire world.

It's hard to imagine anyone including Oswald feeling joy and triumph after assassinating President Kennedy. There were, in November 1963, probably only a handful of men on the face of the earth who would honestly have shared the emotions of triumph over crushing circumstance and oppression, and joy at having at last produced something worthy of the history books. It just happened, as fate so often intercedes in mankind's march toward forever that one such man was close enough, had the skill enough and was frustrated enough to make all our nightmares come true.

1. Michael M. Baden, MD, *Unnatural Death,* (1989, Random House, New York), 10.
2. Ibid., 17.
3. Ibid., 20.
4. Albert H. Newman, *The Assassination of John F. Kennedy—The Reasons Why,* (Clarkson Potter Inc., New York, 1970), 608.
5. Ibid., xi.
6. Bishop, 329.
7. Manchester, 155.
8. WCR, 116.
9. Ibid., 115.
10. Ibid.
11. Ibid., 117.

A Note on Chapter Twelve

Rather than listing references for the subjective reasoning in this chapter, let me direct you to volumes of Hearings Before the President's Commission on the Assassination of President Kennedy, where the testimony of the six eyewitnesses I cite may be found:

Phil Willis, *Hearings VII,* 492-497.

Virgie Baker, *Hearings VII,* 507,515.

Royce Skelton, *Hearings VI,* 236-238.

Jack Franzen, *Hearings XVII,* 840.

Mrs. Franzen, *Hearings XXIV,* 525.

Harry Holmes, *Hearings VII,* 290-292.

CHAPTER

XIII

An Epilogue

I<small>F THE FINAL ANSWER TO THE ASSASSINATION OF PRESIDENT KENNEDY</small> is so patently simple, why have I been the only one to find it? The answer is two-fold. First, my solution depends upon overlooked and ignored eyewitness testimony and a radical new approach to key frames of the Zapruder film. I am not generally an original thinker. These pieces began to fit, for me, only after years of study and research.

Second, most authors and researchers (and the two are often separate) are looking in the wrong direction. Rather than focus on the physical evidence at hand, which would have convicted Oswald in any court of law, they look instead toward the inconsistencies that surround any sort of emotionally charged event. And, since the public still feels sadness, remorse, and rage when the assassination is brought back to the collective consciousness, these writers tend to exploit those feelings for personal and monetary satisfaction, rather than offer a constructive way to lay those wounds aside and move ahead with the problems of life today.

Looking at my bookcase lined with works on the assassination, I count some seventy volumes in my personal collection. This total excludes the HSCA and Warren Commission testimony and exhibits. Now, the interesting statistic: only a half-dozen of those fifty books declare flatly that Oswald was the assassin of President Kennedy. Clearly, there's a buck to be made in bucking the lone assassin theory. And writers know it.

I have chosen to offer a way out of madness. To believe that President Kennedy was killed by a conspiracy is not always to believe in zombie CIA assassins and Watergate burglars on the grassy knoll or in a Secret Service-FBI cover-up, but it is a path to personal doubt and disaster. Only when you and I come to grips with the fact that this mammoth tragedy can, in fact, be blamed on one man, can the personal growth and healing processes begin.

I have watched Robert Groden, Josiah Thompson, G. Robert Blakey and others come to Dealey Plaza. The first thing these writers and researchers always do is look up at that sixth-floor window. If they truly believe Oswald innocent of the assassination, why do they crane their heads to stare upward at the sniper's perch?

The answer is that, deep in the secret recesses of their minds and hearts, nearly all these people accept what will ultimately be history's verdict: Lee Harvey Oswald, acting alone, killed the President. But to show that acceptance would be anathema to the critics, for they have too much at stake. Down the drain would go political causes they champion, money they stand to make, and their personal and professional reputations. Those are hefty reasons for keeping their voices shrill and their platitudes unreasonable.

I am not a rich man. I'm confident that I will be someday, with or without the royalties from this book. I have never made a cent from sensationalizing the assassination. What money I generate from the sale of this book will, to my mind, be payment for years upon years of research, effort, and my desire to set the record straight for the American public.

Skeptics will accuse me of critic-bashing, and I am guilty as charged. But the simple truth is that the critics need to be bashed, by someone who knows what he's talking about. I am that someone. And, since I was a critic once, I know how these professional naysayers work, what they distort, what they overlook and what they have to hide.

The critics have done enough damage to our society. Indeed, it's my belief that they've succeeded in doing something no one should have the right or means to do—they've made us doubt ourselves. Something had to be done.

The problem now is that no one cares. Mention the assassination at a dinner party, a business function, or a social gathering, and see how many people roll their eyes. Each has his or her own preconceived idea of what happened or who was responsible, but all are tired of the subject. They would be content to let it rest.

These are the people who are, quite simply, tired of it all. They are tired of the questions, the accusations, the speculation, and the idle rumor. They are not the people who will buy or read this book. They are destined to go to their graves with unsatisfied curiosity.

And yet, these are the very people my message must somehow reach, for they are the ones who most desperately need to hear what I have to say. The time has come to stop doubting ourselves, our government, and the institutions we have abided by for so long. The time has come to look history in the eye and declare that we know the truth, and that we knew it all along.

For, with a few exceptions in timing and detail, the assassination of President Kennedy was no more than we were told it was. The Warren Commission was right. The House Select Committee, until it allowed itself to be misled, was right as well. Both institutions suffered from a few missing puzzle pieces. Those pieces are presented for the first time in this book.

My case against the critics is clear. I invite them, in any forum, to respond to the questions I've raised in this book.

If a conspiracy assassinated President Kennedy, why have two major, exhaustive investigations conclusively proven otherwise?

Why is there no physical evidence to indicate the presence of a second assassin?

If someone fired at the President from behind the wooden fence atop the grassy knoll, where did the bullet go? Since it didn't strike the President, his companions, or the limousine, what happened to it? Who or where did it hit?

How could a gunman atop the knoll, supposedly a trained marksman shooting at the President of the United States, miss a cross-shot from little more than a hundred feet away?

If more than two bullets struck President Kennedy and Governor Connally, where are the missing fragments? If Oswald was innocent of the assassination, why are the only bullet fragments recovered in this case traceable to his rifle, and only his?

If Oswald didn't bring a paper bag to work on the morning of the assassination, why did witnesses testify to having seen him with it? Did they lie? Why did the bag discovered in the sniper's nest have Oswald's palm print on it?

Where are the curtain rods Oswald must have brought to the Depository, if he wasn't carrying his rifle? Where did they go? Why were they never found?

Why did Oswald hide his clipboard near the stairwell on the sixth floor, without having filled any of the orders on it? Why, if he was innocent, did he apparently spend his morning working hours arranging stacks of book boxes to shield himself from view in the sniper's nest?

Why did he leave behind his wedding ring and nearly all his cash on the morning of the assassination?

Why did Oswald purchase a Coke immediately after the assassination, instead of his usual Dr Pepper?

Why did Oswald, by his own admission, return to his rented room after the assassination and leave with his pistol? Why did he conceal the weapon? Who or what was he running from?

Why did Oswald kill Officer Tippit? And if he didn't, who did? Why are the only cartridge cases recovered at the scene traceable to Oswald's pistol, and no others?

Why did Oswald shout "This is it!" in the Texas Theater, if he didn't expect to be arrested for a crime? Why did he attempt to shoot a policeman there?

Why did Oswald lie to police during his detention?

Why did he deny owning a rifle? Why did he send away for something he claimed not to own? Who removed it from the Paine garage, if not Oswald? Who concealed it on the sixth floor after the assassination, if not Oswald?

If the photos showing Oswald with rifle and pistol in hand were fakes, who faked them? Why did Oswald write on the back of a faked photograph? Why did Marina testify she took them? Why does the one existing negative match Oswald's camera, to the exclusion of all other cameras in the world?

Why do critics never mention that the muzzle velocity of Oswald's rifle exceeds 2,000 feet per second? Why do they never bother to inform their readers that the Mannlicher-Carcano was and is more powerful than any carbine ever used by the United States Army?

Why do they not mention the tests that prove a Mannlicher-Carcano bullet can penetrate two feet of pine and emerge intact? Why do they not mention that the fragments recovered from Governor Connally's wrist have been proven to have come from the stretcher bullet? Why have the critics failed to point out that President Kennedy's hands move from in front of his face to clutch at his throat only after Governor Connally has apparently been hit?

And if the case against Oswald is so shaky, why do the critics resort to blatant misrepresentation of the evidence and photographs?

Why do critics disbelieve Howard Brennen, who insisted that he was too frightened to positively identify Oswald as the man he saw shoot the President, although he was fully able to do so? And what about the witnesses to the Tippit killing? If Oswald wasn't the killer of Officer Tippit, why did a half-dozen eyewitnesses conclusively identify him as the gunman?

If Jack Ruby was a part of a conspiracy to kill Kennedy and murder Oswald, why did he stop at Western Union to send a stripper money, rather than go to the police department basement and wait for Oswald? Why did he leave his beloved dachshund locked in his car, if he believed when he left her that he would be gone for more than a few minutes?

You and I are entitled to additional answers concerning subsequent investigations and the critics' own efforts.

Why did the National Academy of Sciences and the Department of Justice both reject the worthiness of the Dallas Police Dictabelt recording as evidence? Why did the House Select Committee pay so much attention to something so easily demonstrated false?

Why have the critics seen fit to ask question upon countless question, without providing any answers of their own?

If Oswald is innocent, who did shoot President Kennedy and Officer Tippit? Why, after the equivalent of centuries of collective research, have the critics been unable to name names and produce evidence?

Why should we continue to believe individuals who, for their own demonstrable personal gain, continue to decry the dignity of our institutions and leaders, but offer no new solutions of their own?

A quarter-century is too long to be duped, fooled, and mislead by a handful of greedy individuals intent on destroying the credibility of a system many obviously detest. The harm the critics have done to us is reparable, but we must start now.

As Americans, we owe it to President Kennedy and to the idols of truth and justice not to let the naysayers seize the day.

BIBLIOGRAPHY

Anson, Robert Sam. *They've Killed the President!*, New York: Bantam Books, 1975.

Baden, Michael M. *Unnatural Death*, New York: Random House, 1989.

Belin, David W. *November 22, 1963: You Are the Jury*, New York: Quadrangle, 1973.
    Final Disclosure, New York: Charles Scribner's Sons, 1988.

Belli, Melvin. *Dallas Justice*, New York: David McKay Co., 1964.

Bishop, Jim. *The Day Kennedy Was Shot*, New York: Funk & Wagnalls, 1968.

Bloomgarden, Henry S. *The Gun*, New York: Gross Publishers, 1975.

Blumenthal, Sid, and Yazijian, Harvey, Editors. *Government By Gunplay*, New York: New American Library, 1976.

Brennan, Howard, with Cherryholmes, J. Edward. *Eyewitness to History*, Waco, Texas: Texian Press, 1987.

Buchanan, Thomas G. *Who Killed Kennedy?*, New York: G.P. Putnam's Sons, 1964.

Cutler, Robert B, with Morris, W.R. *Alias Oswald*, Manchester, Massachusetts: GKG Partners, 1985.

Donovan, Robert J. *The Assassins*, New York: Harper and Bros. 1964.

Davis, John H. *Mafia Kingfish*, New York: McGraw-Hill, 1989.

Davison, Jean. *Oswald's Game*, New York: W.W. Norton & Co., 1983.

Donnelly, Judy. *Who Shot the President?*, New York: Random House, 1988.

Eddowes, Michael H.B. *Khrushchev Killed Kennedy*, Dallas: Self-Published, 1975.
    The Oswald File, New York: Clarkson N. Potter, 1977.

Epstein, Edward Jay. *Inquest*, New York: Viking Press, 1966.
    Counterplot, New York: Viking Press, 1969
    Legend: The Secret World of Lee Harvey Oswald, New York: McGraw-Hill, 1978.

Evica, George Michael. *And We Are All Mortal*, West Hartford, Connecticut: University of Hartford, 1978.

Fensterwald, Bernard. *Coincidence or Conspiracy?*, New York: Zebra Books, 1977.

Ford, Gerald R. with Stiles, John. *Portrait of the Assassin*, New York: Simon and Schuster, 1965.

Fox, Sylvan. *The Unanswered Questions About President Kennedy's Assassination*, New York: Award Books, 1965.

Garrison, Jim. *Heritage of Stone*, New York: G.P. Putnam's Sons, 1970.
    On the Trail of the Assassins, New York: Sheridan Square Press, 1988.

Gertz, Elmer. *Moment of Madness*, Chicago: Follett Publishing, 1968.

Groden, Robert J., with Model, Peter. *JFK—The Case for Conspiracy*, New York: Manor Books, 1976.

Groden, Robert J. with Livingstone, Harrison E. *High Treason*, Baltimore: Conservatory Press, 1989.

Habe, Hans. *The Wounded Land*, New York: Coward-McCann, 1964.

Hepburn, James. *Farewell America*, Belgium: Frontiers, 1968.

Hurt, Henry. *Reasonable Doubt*, New York: Henry Holt & Co., 1985.

Jovich, John B. *Reflections on JFK's Assassination*, Miami: Woodbine House, 1988.

Joesten, Joachim. *The Biggest Lie Ever Told: The Kennedy Murder Fraud and How I Helped Expose It*, New York: Self-Published, 1968.

Jones, Penn Jr. *Forgive My Grief, Volume One*, Midlothian, Texas: Midlothian Mirror, 1966.
   Forgive My Grief, Volume Two, Midlothian, Texas: Midlothian Mirror,. 1967.
   Forgive My Grief, Volume Three, Midlothian, Texas: Penn Jones Jr., 1976. (Revised Edition)
   Forgive My Grief, Volume Four, Midlothian, Texas: Penn Jones, Jr. 1974.

Kantor, Seth. *Who Was Jack Ruby?*, New York: Everest House, 1978.

Kurtz, Michael. *Crime of the Century*, Knoxville, Tennessee: University of Tennessee Press, 1982.

Lane, Mark. *Rush to Judgment*, New York: Holt, Rinehart and Winston, 1966.
   A Citizen's Dissent, New York: Holt, Rinehart and Winston, 1966.

Lattimer, John K. *Kennedy and Lincoln*, New York: Harcourt Brace Jovanovich, 1980.

Leslie, Warren. *Dallas Public and Private*, New York: Grossman, 1964.

Lewis, Richard W. *The Scavengers and Critics of the Warren Report*, New York: Dell, 1967.

Lifton, David S. *Best Evidence*, New York: Macmillan, 1980.

McDonald, Hugh C., as told to Geoffrey Bocca. *Appointment In Dallas*, New York: Zebra Books, 1975.

McMillan, Priscilla J. *Marina and Lee*, New York: Harper and Row, 1967.

Manchester, William R. *The Death of a President*, New York: Harper and Row, 1967.

Marrs, Jim. *Crossfire*, New York: Carroll & Graf, 1989.

Meagher, Sylvia. *Accessories After the Fact*, New York: Bobbs-Merrill, 1967.

Miller, Tom. *Assassination Please Almanac*, Chicago: Henry Regency, 1977.

Morin, Relman. *Assassination*, New York: New American Library, 1968.

Morrow, Robert D. *Betrayal*, Chicago: Henry Regnery, 1976.

Newman, Albert H. *The Assassination of John F. Kennedy: The Reasons Why*, New York: Clarkston Potter, 1970.

Noyes, Peter. *Legacy of Doubt*, New York: Pinnacle Books, 1973.

Oglesby, Carl. *The Yankee and Cowboy War*, Kansas City: Sheed Andrews and McMeel, 1976.

Oswald, Robert L., with Myrick and Barbara Land. *Lee: A Portrait of Lee Harvey Oswald by His Brother*, New York: Coward-McCann, 1967.

O'Toole, George. *The Assassination Tapes*, New York: Penthouse Press, 1975.

Popkin, Richard. *The Second Oswald*, New York: Avon, 1966.

Roffman, Howard. *Presumed Guilty*, Cranbury, N.J.: Associated University Press, 1975.

Sauvage, Leo. *The Oswald Affair*, Cleveland: World Publishing, 1966.

Scheim, David. *Contract on America*, Silver Spring, Maryland: Argyle Press, 1983.

Scott, Peter Dale, Paul L. Hoch, and Russell Stetler, Editors. *The Assassinations: Dallas and Beyond*, New York: Random House, 1978.

Shaw, J. Gary, with Larry Harris. *Cover-up*, Cleburne, Texas: Shaw, 1976.

Sparrow, John. *After the Assassination*, New York: Chilmark Press, 1967.

Stafford, Jean. *A Mother in History,* New York: Farrar Straus Giroux, 1966.

Summers, Anthony. *Conspiracy,* New York: McGraw-Hill, 1981.

Thompson, Josiah. *Six Seconds in Dallas,* New York: Bernard Geis Associates, 1967.

United Press International. *Four Days,* New York: American Heritage Publishing, 1964.

U. S. House Select Committee on Assassinations. *Hearings Before the Select Committee,* 95th Congress: 2nd Session, 5 Volumes, 1978.

Report of the Select Committee on Assassinations, 95th Congress: 2nd Session, 1978.

U. S. President's Commission on the Assassination of President Kennedy. *Hearings,* 26 Volumes; Washington, D.C.: U. S. Government Printing Office, 1964.

Report of the President's Commission of the Assassination of President Kennedy, Washington, D.C.: U. S. Government Printing Office, 1964.

Weisberg, Harold. *Oswald in New Orleans,* New York: Canyon Books, 1967.

Whitewash, Volumes 1 - 4, Hyattstown, Md: Weisberg, 1965, 1966, 1967, 1974.

Post Mortem, Frederick, Md: Weisberg, 1975.